❊ THE WOODEN SPOON COOKIE BOOK ❊

THE WOODEN SPOON
COOKIE BOOK

Favorite Home-Style Recipes from

The Wooden Spoon Kitchen

MARILYN M. MOORE

THE ATLANTIC MONTHLY PRESS
NEW YORK

Copyright © 1994 by Marilyn M. Moore

Published simultaneously in Canada
Printed in the United States of America

FIRST EDITION

Library of Congress Cataloging-in-Publication Data

Moore, Marilyn M.
The wooden spoon cookie book: favorite home-style recipes from the
wooden spoon kitchen / Marilyn M. Moore.—1st ed.
Includes index.
ISBN 0-87113-601-5
1. Cookies.   I. Title.
TX772.M66   1994   641.8′654—dc20   94-1256

Design by Laura Hammond Hough

The Atlantic Monthly Press
841 Broadway
New York, NY 10003

10 9 8 7 6 5 4 3 2 1

for my grandchildren:

Cynthia, Bonnie, Douglas, Lillian, Rebekah, and Rachel

❈ ACKNOWLEDGMENTS ❈

I had a lot of fun working on this book. As usual, I took baked goodies for tasting to the crew I work with at the library and to the folks who work with my good friend Molly at Flowers and Gifts by Molly Culbert, both located here in my hometown. This time, however, something new was added. During the progress of the manuscript, I had the good fortune to be interviewed for an article in one of our area's most widely read newspapers. The interviewer quoted me as saying that my "friends" were tasting cookies to help select the recipes that would go in the book. I soon had more friends than I had ever imagined.

Molly began passing out tastings to shoppers in her store. The UPS delivery man at the library said that he thought he was a friend of mine, and where were his cookies? I will not attempt to list all of my tasters—I don't even know all of them—but the majority of tasting was done by the following: Lou Graham, Carol Arnold, Scarlet Cropper, Mary Hanson, Donna Judy, Ruth Neathery, and Lupe Ramos at the library; Molly Culbert, James Culbert, Louise Barten, Evelyn

Brown, Judy Custer, Laura Hathaway, Joshua Johnson, Darlene Van Pelt, and Martha Zamarripa at Culbert's; and Jack Van Camp of UPS.

It's always nice to include a recipe from a friend, and for that I wish to thank Bernice Dyck.

❄ CONTENTS ❄

Bar Cookies 59

Shaped Cookies 91

Refrigerator Cookies 123

❊ THE PURE JOY OF COOKIES ❊

Everyone loves homemade cookies. Keep a cookie jar full and you'll tie your apron strings around the hearts of those you share them with. I never have any trouble "getting rid" of cookies. If I want to give any away, I have to move quickly or label them "DO NOT EAT."

Try baking a different kind every week, and take an informal poll of which ones are favorites. My family likes anything with chocolate chips—anything with chocolate, for that matter. (Peanut butter comes in a close second.)

This book has all of our favorites, including quite a few with chocolate chips. Pull up a chair, pour a glass of cold milk, and . . .

Enjoy,
Marilyn M. Moore

❃ KIDS AND COOKIES ❃

Kids love to eat cookies, but more than that, they love to make them. Youngsters can help with the mixing, and they love to roll out the dough and cut out shapes. (Be warned: No one but you will care how much flour gets spilled in the process.) Decorating cookies with store-bought frostings, colored sugars, and/or candies can entertain for a whole morning or afternoon.

When the children are helping, be sure to supervise and be protective around electric appliances, hot ovens, and sharp knives. A kitchen is not a suitable place for unsupervised play. You'll have to be the judge of how much guidance your children need with each baking step. As children learn and mature, you may be able to pull away from direct supervision while keeping a watchful eye.

Remember, too, that youngsters need your presence even more than they need your oversight. It's the time you spend with them, enjoying the fun of baking, that is most important. The skills they learn in the process are secondary.

Special tips for baking with children:

1. Plan ahead for your baking day. Let the kids help decide what you're going to bake, do the shopping for needed ingredients, and get out the utensils you'll be using.
2. Make sure all wash their hands before beginning. Stress the need for cleanliness when working with food.
3. Work at a height that is comfortable for the children. A table top may make a more suitable work area than a counter.
4. Be careful of steps that involve hot or sharp items; assign these to adults or older children.
5. Involve everyone in the clean-up after the baking is over. You may end up doing the bulk of the work, but the children need to learn that clean-up is part of baking day.

❧ HOSTING A HOLIDAY COOKIE SWAP ❧

Winter holidays require cookies, especially at Christmastime. Everyone wants to fill cookie jars and trays with a variety of festive cookies, but few have the time to bake day after day. The solution is to host a cookie swap. There can't be an easier holiday party to have. Try it once and you're likely to turn it into an annual affair.

Gather a few of your friends together for an exchange. If you all have children, it could be a wonderful time for learning some "dress-up" manners. Your children can help with setting the table and serving.

If you have no children at home, you can enliven things by asking a few young parents with children to attend. If you have elderly friends, ask one or two to come to make it an intergenerational gathering. (Be sure to provide transportation for anyone who needs it. Add extra cookies from your kitchen for any guest who doesn't bake.)

Special tips for hosting a cookie swap:

1. Ask each baker to bring six cookies to share with each person attending, including themselves, plus six more for tasting at the party. For

example: If a total of five bakers (including yourself) will attend, each will bring three dozen cookies of one kind.

2. Ask each participant to bring an empty container for taking cookies home. Containers should be clearly marked with the owner's name to avoid confusion as guests depart.

3. As the cookies arrive, ask the guests to help divide the cookies among the marked containers and the "tasting" plates.

4. Serve punch and/or coffee and tea to go with the cookies. Keep things simple. Remember, your guests have brought most of your refreshments.

❊ THE COOKIE KITCHEN ❊

Ingredients
❦

My cookie recipes do not call for exotic ingredients that must be sought out or mail-ordered. Cookies are often spur-of-the-moment decisions, and being able to make them with easily obtainable ingredients is what I consider a plus. You should be able to buy everything you need for the recipes in this book at your local supermarket.

Fats: These recipes use *unsalted butter* and/or *solid vegetable shortening.* The butter is often best for flavor; the shortening is often best for texture. I sometimes combine equal parts of butter and shortening to produce the results I want. Although many bakers use margarine, it is not a perfect substitute for butter since it usually produces a softer dough than butter. I never use butter-flavored shortening; if I want a butter flavor, I use butter. "Whipped," "diet," or "light" spreads cannot be substituted successfully for butter or vegetable shortening. Vegetable oil, a liquid, cannot be substituted for the same amount of solid vegetable shortening. The batter will be thin and will not produce the correct results. Most saturated fats, whether shortening, butter, or margarine, have approximately the same number of calories per tablespoon.

Sweeteners: These recipes call for dry sugars, such as granulated, light brown, or powdered (confectioners'), and liquid sweeteners, such as molasses, corn syrup, or honey. They all have distinct personalities and baking properties. *Granulated sugar* is used most often and it imparts little flavor other than sweetness. *Light brown sugar* has a light molasses flavor. *Powdered sugar* contains a small amount of cornstarch, and I've found that fats do not stay as creamy when it is mixed in. Most powdered sugar is fairly lump-free. If yours has too many lumps, be sure to sift it after measuring. The *molasses* I like to use is unsulphured light molasses, not blackstrap. *Corn syrup* can be light or dark: The dark has a hint of molasses flavor; the light has little taste other than sweet. The *honey* used in these recipes should be a mild honey, such as clover or orange blossom. Dry and liquid sweeteners cannot be substituted for one another with consistent results. Artificial sweeteners cannot be substituted for the real thing with consistent results.

Eggs: The eggs used in testing these recipes were large. Grade AA or Grade A are preferred.

Flour: These recipes call for all-purpose flour, which is available bleached or un-bleached. Although I use unbleached flour for much of my baking, I prefer bleached flour for cookies.

Leavenings: The two leavenings used here are baking powder and baking soda. The *baking powder* should be double-acting (probably the only kind you can find in a supermarket). Baking powder is a combination of baking soda (a base) and cream of tartar (an acid) with a small amount of cornstarch to keep it dry. I prefer a non-aluminum brand, such as Rumford. *Baking soda,* when used alone, reacts with the acids present in the other ingredients of the dough.

Dairy Products: I bake with skim milk, mostly because that is what I have on hand for drinking. It doesn't matter if you use 1%, 2%, or whole milk—use what you have in the refrigerator. The sour cream and cream cheese I use is full-fat. A substitution of lowfat products in recipes that call for these ingredients will not produce the same results.

Chocolate and Cocoa: These recipes call for several types of chocolate: *unsweetened,* in 1-ounce squares; *semisweet,* in 1-ounce squares or in morsels ("chips"); *sweet,* in 1-ounce squares or in morsels; and *cocoa,* in unsweetened powdered form. I prefer Dutch-processed cocoa, sometimes called European-style, because it has been treated with a small amount of alkali to produce a darker, less bitter product. Regular unsweetened cocoa can be substituted with satisfactory results, although the flavor of the finished product may vary.

Salt: I use salt in my cookies for the flavor it imparts. If you wish to avoid salt, the cookies can be made without it.

Flavorings: Use pure (not artificial) flavorings or extracts whenever possible. This is particularly important in the choice of vanilla. Artificial vanilla flavoring is not worthy of your cookie-making efforts.

Nuts: Be sure to use fresh nuts. If you're not sure, taste one before adding them to your dough; a few rancid nuts can ruin an entire batch of cookies. Although the recipes will specify a particular type of nut to use, substitutions can be made without ruining the dough.

Coconut: The coconut used in these recipes is sweetened flaked coconut, easily available in the supermarket, not the shredded kind.

Rolled Oats: The rolled oats (oatmeal) used are old-fashioned or quick-cooking, not instant.

Equipment

You can make stacks of cookies with a minimum of equipment.

Measuring Cups and Spoons: You will need nested cups for measuring dry ingredients, and measuring cups with gradations marked on the sides for measuring liquids. Nested dry measures should include ¼-, ⅓-, ½-, and 1-cup sizes. Measuring spoons should include ¼-, ½-, and 1-teaspoon as well as ½- and 1-tablespoon sizes. If available, a ⅛ cup nested cup and a ⅛ teaspoon measuring spoon are handy to have.

Mixing Bowls and Spoons: I make most of my cookies in the same earthenware bowl and with the same rounded wooden spoon. The bowl has a 3-quart capacity. The spoon is about 12 inches long.

Electric Mixer: An electric mixer can be used in place of a bowl and wooden spoon, but is not necessary.

Food Processor: I sometimes use a food processor for individual steps in the cookie-making process, such as: cutting butter into flour and sugar to produce crumbs, and processing citrus zest with sugar to finely shred. Alternative methods are given for those who do not own this appliance. Some bakers use a food processor to mix cookie dough. I do not.

Baking Sheets: Shiny, heavy-duty, aluminum baking sheets bake excellent cookies, but may need greasing for many recipes. Aluminum baking sheets can be lined with parchment paper to avoid greasing. Avoid dark-colored baking sheets as they absorb heat and can produce cookies with burned bottoms. Nonstick baking sheets can be used if their color is not too dark. I prefer my light-colored nonstick sheets, because I never have to bother with greasing or parchment paper for any of the recipes. Some cookbooks advise against using baking sheets with rims because they claim that rims interfere with air circulation. I use rimmed baking sheets all the time and detect no problem.

Other Baking Pans and Dishes: One 12×9×2-inch glass baking dish; one 8×8×2-inch glass baking dish; and one 15½×10½×1-inch jelly roll pan will take care of baking all of the bar cookies in this book.

Timer: You will need to accurately time your baking. Cookies bake in such a short time that a small variance can make a big difference. I find that a timer that resets automatically to the original setting with the touch of a button is easiest to use.

Rolling Pins and Rolling Surfaces: If you want to make cutout cookies, you will need a rolling pin and a surface on which to roll the dough. Any rolling pin will do as long as you find it comfortable to use; indeed, at a vacation cottage I have successfully used a straight-sided bottle filled with water. The rolling surface can be a bread board or a slab of marble or granite. The advantage to stone surfaces is that the dough will stay cooler and be less sticky to work with. Some bakers use a pastry cloth for rolling out dough. I do not.

Cookie Scoop: A cookie scoop is a neat little device that acts like a spring-loaded ice-cream scoop. One that measures 1 level tablespoon is ideal. When filled level, it is the equivalent of 1 rounded teaspoon; when rounded, it is the equivalent of 1 rounded tablespoon. Available from King Arthur Flour Baker's Catalogue, (800) 827-6836.

Spatulas: You will need a rubber spatula for getting the last bit of dough out of your mixing bowl, and a slanted metal spatula for transferring cookies from baking sheet to cooling racks. A flexible, small metal spatula is good for spreading frostings on baked cookies.

Cooling Racks: If you bake a lot of cookies at a time, you cannot have too many cooling racks. I have one over-size rack and several smaller ones. Although there are some good-looking wooden racks, I prefer metal ones, because they stack compactly in very little of my coveted storage space. Wood also absorbs fats and oils, making racks made of that material unsightly in no time.

Methods
꾟

Cookies are relatively easy to make. There are some procedures, however, that although second nature to the experienced cook, may baffle the novice cookie-baker.

Room Temperature Ingredients: You'll get the best results if all of the ingredients are brought to room temperature before beginning. Since most cookie ingredients are stored at room temperature, this refers primarily to butter and eggs. The butter is best warmed to room temperature by letting it sit on the countertop for an hour or two. If you forget, use your microwave. *To soften butter in a microwave oven:* Cut one stick of butter into 4 pieces and place them in a glass measuring cup. Microwave on high power for 20 to 30 seconds, depending on your oven (the higher the wattage, the less time needed), until just beginning to soften. Beat with a wooden spoon or mixer to complete the softening.

Because of possible salmonella contamination, I don't advise leaving eggs out for extended periods of time. They can be warmed quickly by immersing them in a small container of warm water. A cold egg can "curdle" a previously smooth blend of butter and sugar, but I have added cold eggs to my butter-sugar mixtures when in a hurry. I simply beat the eggs, on one side of the bowl, with a small portion of the butter-sugar mixture until smooth, and then beat that into the remainder.

Measuring Brown Sugar: Brown sugar should be packed into a measuring cup or spoon before leveling off to measure.

"Creaming" or Blending the Butter and the Sugar: In the first step of cookie making, the butter or shortening is "creamed," or beaten with the sugar, until the mixture is smooth and creamy. Better yet, beat the shortening or butter until creamy before adding any sugar to it.

Adding Eggs and Flavorings: Unless otherwise specified in the recipe, when the eggs and flavorings are added to a batter or dough, they need to be beaten only until the mixture is well blended.

Measuring and Adding Flour: It is important to measure flour accurately. Do not sift it first; instead, spoon it lightly into a dry measure and then level off with a straight edge. Do not pack it into the cup or scoop it up with the cup itself. Sifting flour before measuring results in a smaller measure of flour; packing it into the cup results in too much. Since flour makes up such a high proportion of the cookie dough, accuracy in measurement is critical. These recipes don't require sifting at all. If lumps need to be removed, a simple stir will mix them sufficiently for adding to the dough. Once all of the flour is added to a cookie dough, beat only enough to blend the ingredients thoroughly. Overbeating at this stage can produce tough cookies. If the dough appears too sticky after mixing, chill the dough before adding more flour. It may not need any extra after it's cold.

Adding Cocoa: To avoid "lumping," always stir cocoa with sugar or flour before adding it to a batter. Cocoa that is added alone tends to lump, and once those lumps get wet, they are very hard to break up.

Melting Chocolate: Chocolate can be melted in the top of a double boiler over hot, not boiling, water. Take care not to get any water or steam into the melting chocolate, or it will "seize up," turning thick and grainy. Leave the melted chocolate over the warm water, off the heat, until ready to use. Stir and use slightly warm, but not hot, when adding to doughs.

 To melt chocolate in a microwave oven: Use high power, allowing 45 seconds for 1 square, and adding 15 seconds for each additional square. Chocolate melted this way may hold its shape until stirred. If you choose the microwave method, remember that chocolate can become overcooked or scorched in that appliance just as easily as on stovetop. Take it easy. Chocolate can also be melted in a heavy saucepan, directly over low heat, stirring constantly. This method bears more constant watching to avoid scorching or burning.

Greasing Baking Sheets: When greasing a baking sheet for cookie-baking, use only a very thin layer of shortening; too much can cause the cookies to spread farther than intended. The best way to grease is to pick up a dab of shortening with a folded paper napkin and rub it over the surface of the baking sheet. Refold the napkin and remove any excess grease with a dry portion of the napkin. Nonstick baking sheets may require greasing if the nonstick coating is damaged or beginning to wear out.

Forming Cookies: Whether dropping dough from a spoon, forming shapes with your hands, or rolling out and cutting dough, it is important to make cookies that will be baked together the same size as each other so that all can bake in the same amount of time. A sheet of some small, some medium, and some huge cookies virtually guarantees some that are over- or under-cooked.

Drop cookies should be pushed off the spoon with another spoon or with your fingers. The spoon to use is tableware, not measuring. *Shaped cookies* are formed with your hands as directed in the recipe. *Cutout cookies* are cut from chilled dough that is rolled out to a uniform thickness.

Rolling out cookie dough: Try not to work excessive amounts of flour into the dough as it is rolled. Take the specified amount of dough and shape it in your hands to a flattened ball. Dust the rolling surface lightly with flour. Press the dough into this flour and then pick it back up. Dust the surface again and press the other side of the dough into the flour. Begin rolling out from the center to the outside edges, dusting the surface only when necessary to prevent sticking. The dough can be turned over once or twice more before it becomes too large to make it easy to flip. Measure the depth of the rolled out dough to make sure it corresponds to the recipe.

To cut out shapes: Dip cookie cutters into flour as often as needed to prevent sticking. When all are cut, pull away the excess dough between the cut-outs and stockpile for re-rolls. Slip a metal spatula underneath each cookie to aid in transfer. I hold the spatula in my right hand, transfer the loosened cookie from the spatula to my left hand, and lay the cookie on the baking sheet with my left hand. There is less distortion of shape with this method than with direct transfer from spatula to sheet.

When making cutout cookies, the first ones you roll and cut will be more tender than those re-rolled from the scraps of dough left from the first go-round. This is because the re-rolled dough picks up extra flour from the rolling surface. I sometimes gather up the scraps and knead them gently into a log, which I wrap with waxed paper or plastic wrap and refrigerate. Then I slice and bake the dough as refrigerator cookies on a later day. If you do re-roll your scraps, you might want to store and mark the baked cookies separately. At our house we would serve the better cookies to company and eat the re-rolls ourselves.

Baking: Arrange the oven racks the way you want them before preheating. Place the oven rack in the center position for baking one sheet of cookies at a time. Preheat the oven before baking. A too-low temperature will begin to melt the cookie dough before it is baked. Be sure the baking sheets are cool before the second batch is placed on them to avoid the same kind of melt-down.

My mother used to use two racks and bake two sheets of cookies at a time. By the time she had the second sheet ready to go in the oven, she switched the first sheet from the bottom rack to the top, reversing it back to front as she did so. When the next was ready, she took out the first, switched the second, and inserted the third. I prefer my more leisurely method of one at a time. If you wish to follow in my mother's footsteps, you will have to position one rack one-third from the top and another one-third from the bottom of the oven, and you will have to add an undetermined number of minutes to the baking time specified in the recipe (to compensate for heat lost while the oven door is open).

Cooling the Cookies: Using a metal spatula, transfer baked cookies to wire racks to cool. Fragile cookies may need to rest a minute before removal. If you wait too long and the cookies stick, they can be returned to the oven for a minute and

rewarmed. Do not stack warm cookies on top of one another. If you lack suffi-
cient racks for cooling, place them directly on a clean countertop.

Storing Cookies: Make sure the cookies are completely cool before storing. Store
all individual cookies in airtight containers, such as cookie jars with close-fitting
lids or sealed plastic bags. Store soft and crisp cookies separately. Bar cookies can
be stored, tightly covered, in the pan in which they were baked. Cookies that
require refrigeration should be covered tightly, lest they absorb odors from other
foods. Decorated or sticky cookies should be stored in a single layer. If you need
to stack them, separate the layers with sheets of waxed paper. Crisp cookies that
have softened can be recrisped in a 300°F oven for 3 to 5 minutes. Cool on a rack
after crisping.

Refrigerating and Freezing Cookie Dough and Cookies: Most cookies will stay
palatably fresh at room temperature for about a week. Freezing will prolong
freshness for up to 3 months. Make sure cookies to be frozen are packed airtight,
in freezer-weight plastic bags, or double-wrapped in foil. Expel as much air as
possible. Rigid plastic containers should be used for fragile cookies. Soft cookies
or decorated cookies can be frozen uncovered on trays and packaged after frozen
hard. Wrap, label, and return to the freezer. Always label containers of cookies
with a piece of tape giving the name of the cookie, quantity, and date of storage.
Defrost cookies before unwrapping. A small plateful of frozen cookies can be
covered loosely with a paper towel and "zapped" in a microwave for 10 seconds
to speed the process.

Most unbaked cookie doughs can be covered and refrigerated for up to a
week. Bring to room temperature before shaping and baking. Frozen dough will

keep for up to 2 months. Thaw frozen dough in the refrigerator overnight before forming and baking. Refrigerator cookies, however, can be sliced from a frozen log as soon as thawed enough to do so.

Gift-wrapping Cookies: Food companies will, from time to time, package goods in quaint or commemorative containers. I always buy and save these for packaging cookies for gifting. Second-hand shops, garage sales, and flea markets are good sources for used tins, baskets, and cookie jars. For a carry-in gift, line an attractive basket with a cloth or paper napkin and fill to overflowing with homemade cookies. An index card giving the recipe for the cookie makes a nice touch. For a special present, package your cookies with the pan in which they would be baked and include a cookie cookbook.

Packing and Mailing Cookies: You want your cookies to arrive in perfect condition, not as a box of crumbs. Sturdy bar cookies and drop cookies ship the best. Avoid fragile, thin cookies and those with frostings. Never mail a cookie that requires refrigeration to store.

Always wrap soft and crisp cookies separately to preserve their character and texture. Cookies can be wrapped in plastic in small stacks, or in pairs, flat sides together. Sharon Tyler Herbst suggests in her book *The Joy of Cookies* that if the cookies are the right size, they can be attractively stacked inside paper cupcake liners. Always place the heaviest cookies on the bottom of the container. Crumple waxed paper to pad the top and fill the headroom of the container.

Pack a container of cookies in a box that allows room on all sides for a cushion of filler. Use crumpled paper, reusable bubble-wrap, or ecologically correct biodegradable plastic "popcorn" for cushioning. Pad the bottom of the box with several inches of filler. Place the container of cookies in the center, and fill the remaining space on the sides and top with additional filler. Seal the box securely with package-sealing tape or strapping tape. Do not use string (string can catch in the shipper's handling machinery). Clearly print your return address and shipping address on the box or attach a typed shipping label. Cover the address or label with clear tape. Ship by overnight, two-day, or first-class mail to get your cookies to their destination as soon as possible.

❊ FILLING THE COOKIE JAR ❊

❅ DROP COOKIES ❅

Drop cookies are the most popular cookies of all, probably because they are so easy and quick to stir up. The doughs welcome additions of fruits, nuts, and cereals, giving them a wide variety of tastes, textures, and appearances.

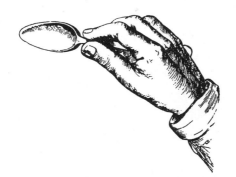

❋ Soft Sugar Cookies ❋

Soft sugar cookies are as old-fashioned as Victorian lace. Serve them on your finest china with an afternoon cup of tea.

YIELD: 4 DOZEN 2-INCH COOKIES

½ cup (1 stick) unsalted butter, softened
½ cup granulated sugar
½ cup powdered sugar
1 large egg
½ teaspoon vanilla extract
1½ cups all-purpose flour
½ teaspoon baking powder
½ teaspoon baking soda
¼ teaspoon salt
¼ teaspoon ground nutmeg
½ cup buttermilk

FROSTING:
2 cups powdered sugar
2 tablespoons unsalted butter, softened
1 teaspoon vanilla extract
2 to 3 tablespoons buttermilk

1. Preheat the oven to 350°F. Lightly grease 2 baking sheets, or use non-stick pans.

2. Beat the butter with the granulated sugar until soft and creamy. Add the powdered sugar and beat again. Add the egg and vanilla and beat until smooth. Stir together the flour, baking powder, baking soda, salt, and nutmeg. Add alternately to the butter mixture with the buttermilk, beginning and ending with the dry ingredients (3 parts dry ingredients, 2 parts buttermilk), until well mixed.

3. Drop the dough by rounded teaspoonfuls onto the baking sheets, leaving 2 inches between the drops. Bake for 9 to 10 minutes, or until just the bottoms are lightly browned. The tops of the cookies should remain pale. Transfer to wire racks to cool.

4. To prepare the frosting: In a small bowl, blend the powdered sugar, butter, and vanilla. Gradually add the buttermilk until the mixture is spreadable. Frost the cookies when they have cooled to room temperature.

❧ Sugar-Glazed Chocolate Chip Cookies ❧

I use a little less sugar in this cookie batter than you usually find, and sprinkle just a tad on the tops right before baking. That simple sugar glaze transforms them from something ordinary into something quite good.

YIELD: 5 DOZEN 2¼-INCH COOKIES

½ cup solid vegetable shortening
½ cup (1 stick) unsalted butter, softened
⅔ cup plus 1 tablespoon granulated sugar
⅔ cup firmly packed light brown sugar
1 teaspoon vanilla extract
2 large eggs
2¼ cups all-purpose flour
1 teaspoon baking soda
1 teaspoon salt
1 tablespoon milk
2 cups (12 ounces) semisweet chocolate morsels
½ cup chopped walnuts (optional)

1. Preheat the oven to 375°F. Lightly grease 2 baking sheets, or use non-stick pans.

2. Beat the shortening with the butter until smooth and creamy. Add ⅔ cup of the granulated sugar and beat again. Add the brown sugar and beat again. Beat in the vanilla and the eggs. Stir together the flour, baking soda, and salt. Stir

half of the flour mixture into the dough. Stir in the milk, and then the remaining flour mixture. Stir in the chocolate morsels and nuts.

3. Drop the dough by heaping teaspoonfuls onto the baking sheets, leaving 2 inches between the drops. Sprinkle the tops with the remaining 1 tablespoon sugar, using about ½ teaspoon sugar for each dozen cookies. Bake for 8 to 10 minutes, or until golden brown on top. Transfer to wire racks to cool.

Peanut Butter–Chocolate Chip Cookies

Follow the recipe for Sugar-Glazed Chocolate Chip Cookies. Add ½ cup creamy peanut butter and 1 tablespoon honey when you add the vanilla and eggs. Substitute dry-roasted peanuts for the walnuts.

❀ Sugar Drops ❀

These classic cookies appeared in many early cookbooks. They were basic drop cookies that took well to the addition of chopped nuts or dried fruit. Then one historic day, Ruth Wakefield of the Toll House Inn added chopped chocolate to her Sugar Drops. The recipe was so popular that it was eventually sold to Nestlé and published as the Original Toll House Chocolate Chip Cookies. Here is my version of the original without Wakefield's innovation. I particularly like these with 1 cup each of walnuts and apricots.

YIELD: 4 DOZEN 2½-INCH COOKIES

1 cup (2 sticks) unsalted butter, softened
¾ cup granulated sugar
¾ cup firmly packed light brown sugar
2 large eggs
1 teaspoon vanilla extract
2¼ cups all-purpose flour
1 teaspoon salt
1 teaspoon baking soda
2 cups chopped nuts or dried fruit

1. Preheat the oven to 375°F. Use ungreased baking sheets.

2. Beat the butter with both sugars until blended. Add the eggs and vanilla and beat again. Stir the flour with the salt and baking soda; stir this mixture into the batter. Stir in the nuts or fruit.

3. Use a tablespoon to scoop out 1½-inch globs of the dough and push onto the baking sheets, leaving 2 inches between the globs. Bake for 9 to 10 minutes, or until lightly browned with no obvious white spots on the tops. Transfer to wire racks to cool.

Classic Chocolate Chip Cookies

Substitute 2 cups (one 12-ounce package) semisweet chocolate morsels for the nuts or fruit in Sugar Drops.

❀ Chocolate Chunk Cookies ❀

Chunks of semisweet chocolate melt here and there throughout these delicate little cookies. The cocoa used is Dutch-processed, which produces a chocolate flavor with no bitter aftertaste. These cookies are heaven.

YIELD: 3 DOZEN 2½-INCH COOKIES

½ cup (1 stick) unsalted butter, softened
¾ cup granulated sugar
1 teaspoon vanilla extract
1 large egg
1 cup all-purpose flour
2 tablespoons Dutch-processed unsweetened cocoa powder
½ teaspoon baking soda
½ teaspoon salt
8 squares (1-ounce each) semisweet chocolate, cut into ¼-inch chunks (It's okay if the chunks vary in size.)

1. Preheat the oven to 375°F. Lightly grease 2 baking sheets, or use non-stick pans.

2. Beat together the butter and sugar until soft and creamy. Blend in the vanilla, and then the egg. Stir together the flour, cocoa, baking soda, and salt; blend into the butter mixture. Stir in the chopped chocolate.

3. Drop the dough by rounded teaspoonfuls onto the baking sheets, leaving 2 inches between the drops. Bake for 10 to 12 minutes, or until lightly browned on the edges. Transfer to wire racks to cool.

❀ Vanilla Chip Cookies ❀

These cookies have a satisfying vanilla flavor that's like a good French vanilla ice cream. In fact, the two go together remarkably well.

YIELD: 4 DOZEN 2½-INCH COOKIES

¾ cup (1 ½ sticks) unsalted butter, softened
¾ cup granulated sugar
¾ cup firmly packed light brown sugar
2 large eggs
1 tablespoon vanilla extract
2 ¼ cups all-purpose flour
½ teaspoon salt
½ teaspoon baking soda
1 package (10 ounces) vanilla milk chips
1 cup chopped pecans

1. Preheat the oven to 375°F. Lightly grease 2 baking sheets, or use non-stick pans.

2. Beat the butter until smooth and creamy. Add both sugars and beat again. Add the eggs, one at a time, beating well after each addition. Stir in the vanilla. Stir together the flour, salt, and baking soda; stir into the dough. Stir in the vanilla chips and pecans.

3. Drop 1½-inch globs of dough onto the baking sheets, leaving 2 inches between the globs. Bake for about 10 minutes, or until lightly browned. Transfer to wire racks to cool.

❦ Chocolate Clusters ❦

Don't overbake these and you will be rewarded with soft and chewy cookies filled with chocolate, walnuts, and a pleasant surprise—raisins. The baking sheets should be nonstick or parchment paper–lined for ease of cookie removal.

YIELD: 5 DOZEN 3-INCH COOKIES

2 cups (12 ounces) semisweet chocolate morsels
1 cup (2 sticks) unsalted butter, softened
1½ cups granulated sugar
1 teaspoon vanilla extract
2 large eggs
2½ cups all-purpose flour
1 teaspoon salt
1 teaspoon baking soda
1 cup chopped walnuts
1 cup raisins

1. Preheat the oven to 375°F. Use nonstick or parchment-lined baking sheets.

2. Melt 1 cup of the chocolate morsels and set aside to cool until just slightly warm.

3. Beat the butter until smooth and creamy. Add the sugar and beat again. Stir in the vanilla. Add the eggs, one at a time, beating well after each

addition. Stir in the melted chocolate. Stir together the flour, salt, and baking soda; stir into the dough. Stir in the walnuts, raisins, and the remaining 1 cup chocolate morsels.

4. Drop 1½-inch globs of dough onto the baking sheets, leaving 2 inches between the globs. Bake for 8 to 10 minutes, or until the tops of the cookies are soft but the bottoms are set. Transfer to wire racks to cool.

❊ Brown Sugar–Pecan Cookies ❊

These simple cookies are rich with brown sugar, butter, and pecans. One of my favorites.

YIELD: 4 DOZEN 2½-INCH COOKIES

1 cup (2 sticks) unsalted butter, softened
1 cup firmly packed light brown sugar
2 large eggs
1 teaspoon vanilla extract
2 cups all-purpose flour
¼ teaspoon salt
2 teaspoons baking powder
1 cup finely chopped pecans

1. Preheat the oven to 350°F. Use ungreased baking sheets.

2. Beat the butter until soft and creamy. Add the brown sugar and beat again. Stir in the eggs and vanilla. Stir together the flour, salt, and baking powder; stir into the dough. Stir in the pecans.

3. Drop 1½-inch globs of dough onto the baking sheets, leaving 2 inches between the globs. Bake for 9 to 11 minutes, or until little or no depression remains when the cookies are touched lightly in the center. Cool on wire racks.

❧ Gumdrop Cookies ❧

I like gumdrops, so I have to watch that I don't eat too many while I'm snipping them up for this recipe. You'll want to use nonstick or parchment-lined pans for these—the gumdrops have a tendency to stick, and greasing the pan makes the cookies spread too much.

YIELD: 3 DOZEN 2½-INCH COOKIES

½ cup vegetable shortening
1 cup granulated sugar
½ teaspoon orange extract
1 large egg
3 tablespoons milk
1¾ cups all-purpose flour
¼ teaspoon salt
½ teaspoon baking soda
1½ cups small spice gumdrops (no licorice), snipped crosswise into fourths

1. Preheat the oven to 375°F. Use nonstick or parchment-lined baking sheets.

2. Beat the shortening and sugar together until well blended. Add the orange extract, egg, and milk and beat again. Stir together the flour, salt, and baking soda; stir into the dough. Stir in the gumdrops.

3. Drop the dough by rounded teaspoonfuls onto the baking sheets, leaving 2 inches between the drops. Bake for 9 to 11 minutes, or until almost no depression remains when the cookies are lightly touched in the center. Transfer to wire racks to cool.

❧ Chocolate Drops ❧

My family loves chocolate drops. These are dark, chocolaty, and cake-like, with the surprise of chocolate chips.

YIELD: 5 DOZEN 2-INCH COOKIES

½ cup solid vegetable shortening
½ cup granulated sugar
½ cup firmly packed light brown sugar
1 teaspoon vanilla extract
2 large eggs
1½ cups all-purpose flour
½ teaspoon salt
1 teaspoon baking soda
½ cup Dutch-processed unsweetened cocoa powder
½ cup milk
2 cups (12 ounces) semisweet chocolate morsels

1. Preheat the oven to 375°F. Lightly grease 2 baking sheets, or use nonstick pans.

2. Beat the shortening and granulated sugar together until blended. Add the brown sugar and beat again. Add the vanilla and eggs and beat until light and fluffy. Stir the flour, salt, baking soda, and cocoa together. Add the dry ingredients alternately with the milk (3 parts dry ingredients, 2 parts milk), until well mixed. Stir in the chocolate morsels.

3. Drop the dough by rounded teaspoonfuls onto the baking sheets, leaving 2 to 3 inches between the drops. Bake for 10 to 12 minutes, or until the tops of the cookies spring back when lightly touched; they should not brown. Cool on wire racks.

❋ Poppy-Seeded Lemon Drops ❋

These are slightly chewy with the sybaritic flavor combination of lemon and poppy seeds.

YIELD: 3½ DOZEN 2½-INCH COOKIES

¾ cup (1½ sticks) unsalted butter, softened
1½ cups granulated sugar
1 large egg
1 teaspoon lemon extract
1¾ cups all-purpose flour
¼ teaspoon baking powder
¼ teaspoon salt
2 tablespoons poppy seeds

1. Preheat the oven to 350°F. Lightly grease 2 baking sheets, or use non-stick pans.

2. Beat together the butter and sugar until soft and creamy. Add the egg and lemon extract and blend well. Stir together the flour, baking powder, salt, and poppy seeds; blend into the creamed mixture.

3. Drop the dough by rounded teaspoonfuls onto the baking sheets, leaving 2 inches between the drops. Bake for 10 to 12 minutes, or until lightly browned around the edges. Transfer to wire racks to cool.

❈ Honey-Walnut Cookies ❈

These will spread, making a chewy cookie that's filled with walnuts and the flavor of honey.

YIELD: 3 DOZEN 2½-INCH COOKIES

½ cup (1 stick) unsalted butter, softened
½ cup granulated sugar
½ cup honey
1 large egg
1¾ cups all-purpose flour
¼ teaspoon salt
½ teaspoon baking soda
¾ cup finely chopped walnuts

1. Preheat the oven to 375°F. Lightly grease 2 baking sheets, or use non-stick pans.

2. Beat the butter and sugar together until well blended. Add the honey and beat again. Beat in the egg. Stir together the flour, salt, and baking soda; stir into the dough. Stir in the walnuts.

3. Drop the dough by rounded teaspoonfuls onto the baking sheets, leaving 2 inches between the drops. Bake for 8 to 10 minutes, or until browned on top. Let rest on the baking sheet for 1 minute before removing to wire racks to cool.

❀ Cream Cheese Cookies ❀

These are rich, slightly chewy, pecan-filled cookies. I like them with a fruit salad for lunch.

YIELD: 3 DOZEN 2-INCH COOKIES

½ cup (1 stick) unsalted butter, softened
1 small package (3 ounces) cream cheese, softened
1 cup granulated sugar
½ teaspoon vanilla extract
1 teaspoon milk
pinch of salt
1 cup all-purpose flour
½ cup finely chopped pecans

1. Preheat the oven to 375°F. Use ungreased baking sheets.

2. Beat the butter with the cream cheese until smooth and creamy. Add the sugar and beat again. Stir in the vanilla, milk, and salt. Stir in the flour, and then the pecans.

3. Drop the dough by teaspoonfuls onto the baking sheets, leaving 2 inches between the drops. Bake for about 10 minutes, or until browned around the edges; the centers will still be slightly soft. Let the cookies rest on the cookie sheets for 1 minute before transferring to wire racks to cool.

❧ Lunch Box Oatmeal Cookies ❧

These are satisfyingly chewy—like the ones Grandma used to make.

YIELD: 3 DOZEN 2¾-INCH COOKIES

1 cup solid vegetable shortening
¾ cup granulated sugar
¾ cup firmly packed light brown sugar
2 large eggs
1 teaspoon vanilla extract
2 tablespoons fresh orange juice
1½ cups all-purpose flour
1 teaspoon salt
1 teaspoon baking soda
1 teaspoon ground cinnamon
3 cups quick or old-fashioned rolled oats (not instant)
1 cup raisins

1. Preheat the oven to 350°F. Use ungreased baking sheets.

2. Beat together the shortening and granulated sugar until smooth and creamy. Add the brown sugar and beat again. Blend in the eggs, and then the vanilla and orange juice. Stir together the flour, salt, baking soda, and cinnamon; stir into the batter. Add the oats and raisins and stir to mix.

3. Use a tablespoon to scoop out 1½-inch globs of dough and push them onto the baking sheets, leaving 2 inches between the globs. Bake for 12 to 14 minutes, or until lightly, but evenly, browned. Transfer to wire racks to cool.

❧ Soft Raisin Cookies ❧

These are old-fashioned boiled raisin cookies. Boiling brings out the sweetness of the raisins while it plumps them. Mmmmm, they are good.

YIELD: 5 DOZEN 2¾-INCH COOKIES

1 cup raisins
¾ cup water
½ cup solid vegetable shortening
½ cup (1 stick) unsalted butter, softened
2 cups granulated sugar
3 large eggs
1 teaspoon vanilla extract
3½ cups all-purpose flour
1 teaspoon salt
1 teaspoon baking powder
1 teaspoon baking soda
1 teaspoon ground cinnamon
¼ teaspoon ground nutmeg
¼ teaspoon ground cloves

1. In a small saucepan, gently boil the raisins in the water for 5 minutes. Set aside to cool. (You can refrigerate them to speed the cooling process.)

2. Preheat the oven to 350°F. Lightly grease 2 baking sheets, or use non-stick pans.

3. Beat together the shortening and butter until smooth and creamy. Add the sugar and beat again. Beat in the eggs, one at a time. Blend in the vanilla. Stir together the flour, salt, baking powder, baking soda, cinnamon, nutmeg, and cloves. Stir half of the dry ingredients into the batter; stir in the cooled raisin mixture, and then stir in the remaining dry ingredients.

4. Drop the dough by heaping teaspoonfuls onto the prepared baking sheets, leaving 2 inches between the drops. Bake for 10 to 12 minutes, or until very lightly, but evenly, browned. Cool on wire racks.

❦ Banana Cookies ❦

We always have a few bananas that wait too long to be eaten out of hand. That's when we make Banana Cookies. These have a nice light texture and the flavor of banana nut bread.

YIELD: 5 DOZEN 2½-INCH COOKIES

½ cup (1 stick) unsalted butter, softened
½ cup solid vegetable shortening
¾ cup granulated sugar
¾ cup firmly packed light brown sugar
2 large eggs
1 teaspoon vanilla extract
2¼ cups all-purpose flour
½ teaspoon salt
1 teaspoon baking soda
1 teaspoon ground cinnamon
¼ teaspoon ground nutmeg
1 cup mashed banana (2 large)
1 cup chopped pecans

1. Preheat the oven to 375°F. Lightly grease 2 baking sheets, or use non-stick pans.

2. Beat the butter and shortening with both sugars until smooth and creamy. Beat in the eggs, and then the vanilla. Stir together the flour, salt, baking

soda, cinnamon, and nutmeg; stir half of this mixture into the dough. Stir in the banana, and then the remaining flour mixture. Stir in the pecans.

3. Use a teaspoon to scoop up 1¼-inch round globs of the dough and push them onto the baking sheets, leaving 2 inches between the globs. Bake for 8 to 10 minutes, or until the cookies are lightly, but evenly, browned. Transfer to wire racks to cool.

❄ Molasses-Ginger Cookies ❄

The flavor of these cookies will remind you of old-fashioned gingerbread.

YIELD: 3 DOZEN 2½-INCH COOKIES

½ cup solid vegetable shortening
½ cup firmly packed light brown sugar
1 large egg
1 cup molasses
2½ cups all-purpose flour
¼ teaspoon salt
1 teaspoon baking soda
1 teaspoon ground ginger
¼ teaspoon ground cloves
¼ teaspoon ground nutmeg
½ cup lowfat buttermilk

1. Preheat the oven to 375°F. Lightly grease 2 baking sheets, or use non-stick pans.

2. Beat together the shortening and brown sugar until smooth and creamy. Blend in the egg, and then the molasses. Stir together the flour, salt, baking soda, ginger, cloves, and nutmeg. Stir half of the dry ingredients into the batter; stir in the buttermilk, and then the remaining dry ingredients.

3. Use a teaspoon to scoop up 1½-inch globs of the dough and push them onto the prepared baking sheets, leaving 2 inches between globs. Bake for

10 to 12 minutes, or just until the tops of the cookies spring back when lightly touched in the center; the cookies should not brown. Let rest for 1 minute before removing from the baking sheets. Cool on wire racks.

❊ Juneberry Cookies ❊

The berries for these cookies come from the Juneberry tree (aka Serviceberry, Sarvis tree, Shadblow). The trees can be found in the undergrowth of mixed deciduous woods. (For identification, I suggest: *An Instant Guide to Edible Plants* by Pamela Forey and Cecilia Fitzsimons, Crescent Books, 1989.) The fruits ripen in mid- to late summer, first turning bright red, and then purple. It is when they are purple that they should be picked. If you can't find Juneberries, you can substitute blueberries. Select undersized berries rather than plump ones, as the Juneberries they are replacing are but ⅜ inch in diameter.

YIELD: 4 DOZEN 2-INCH COOKIES

½ cup (1 stick) unsalted butter, softened
1¼ cups granulated sugar
1 large egg
½ teaspoon lemon extract
2 cups all-purpose flour
½ teaspoon salt
1½ teaspoons baking powder
¼ cup milk
1 cup Juneberries, washed and well-drained
powdered sugar, for dusting the cookies

1. Preheat the oven to 375°F. Lightly grease 2 baking sheets, or use non-stick pans.

2. Beat the butter with the sugar until smooth and creamy. Add the egg and lemon extract and beat well. Stir together the flour, salt, and baking powder; add alternately with the milk (3 parts dry ingredients, 2 parts milk), until well mixed. Gently stir in the berries.

3. Drop the dough by rounded teaspoonfuls onto the baking sheets, leaving 2 inches between the drops. Bake for 10 to 12 minutes, or until golden on top. Transfer to wire racks to cool. Sift a light dusting of powdered sugar over the cookies before they are completely cool.

❧ Pineapple Cookies ❧

These have a good pineapple character, enhanced by the juice-flavored glaze.

YIELD: 4 DOZEN 2-INCH COOKIES

1 can (8 ounces) crushed pineapple, packed in juice
½ cup (1 stick) unsalted butter, softened
1 cup granulated sugar
½ cup firmly packed light brown sugar
2 large eggs
½ teaspoon vanilla extract
½ teaspoon orange extract
2¾ cups all-purpose flour
½ teaspoon salt
1 teaspoon baking soda

GLAZE:
2 cups powdered sugar
¼ cup (½ stick) unsalted butter, softened

1. Preheat the oven to 350°F. Lightly grease 2 baking sheets, or use non-stick pans.

2. Drain the pineapple, reserving the juice for the glaze. Beat the butter with both sugars until blended. Add the eggs and beat again. Add both extracts

and beat again. Stir in the drained pineapple. Combine the flour, salt, and baking soda; stir into the batter.

3. Drop the dough by rounded teaspoonfuls onto the baking sheets, leaving 2 inches between the drops. Bake for 10 minutes, or until golden on top. Transfer to wire racks to cool.

4. To prepare the glaze: Beat the powdered sugar with the butter until blended. Gradually add 3 to 4 tablespoons of the reserved pineapple juice and mix until the mixture is spreadable. When the cookies are cool, use a pastry brush to brush each cookie with the glaze.

❀ Coconut Cookies ❀

These are sweet little cookies with just the right amount of coconut to please.

YIELD: 3 DOZEN 2¼-INCH COOKIES

½ cup (1 stick) unsalted butter, softened
½ cup granulated sugar
½ cup firmly packed light brown sugar
1 large egg
1½ teaspoons vanilla extract
1½ cups all-purpose flour
¼ teaspoon salt
½ teaspoon baking soda
2 tablespoons lowfat buttermilk
1 cup sweetened flaked coconut

1. Preheat the oven to 350°F. Lightly grease 2 baking sheets, or use non-stick pans.

2. Beat the butter with the granulated sugar until smooth and creamy. Add the brown sugar and beat again. Beat in the egg, and then the vanilla. Stir together the flour, salt, and baking soda. Stir half of this mixture into the dough; stir in the buttermilk, and then the remaining flour mixture. Stir in the coconut.

3. Drop the dough by rounded teaspoonfuls onto the baking sheets, leaving 2 inches between the drops. Bake for 10 to 12 minutes, or until golden brown on top. Transfer to wire racks to cool.

❋ BAR COOKIES ❋

Bar cookies are great for the cook on the go. No time need be spent on shaping individual cookies, and all are baked at once. Transportation is easy—they can be carried in the same pan they were baked in.

❧ Little Brownie Bars ❧

These have a fudgy texture that's irresistible. They're cut small so you don't have to feel guilty about enjoying one.

YIELD: 32 BARS, 1×2 INCHES EACH

2 squares (1 ounce each) unsweetened chocolate
½ cup (1 stick) unsalted butter
1 cup granulated sugar
2 large eggs
½ teaspoon vanilla extract
¼ teaspoon salt
⅓ cup all-purpose flour
sifted powdered sugar, for coating the bars

1. Preheat the oven to 325°F. Grease an 8×8×2-inch glass baking dish.

2. In a glass bowl, microwave the chocolate with the butter on high power for 1 to 1½ minutes. Stir to finish melting the chocolate. (Alternatively: Melt the chocolate with the butter in a heavy saucepan over low heat, stirring constantly.)

3. Using whatever container the chocolate and butter were melted in, stir in the sugar. Add the eggs, one at a time, beating well after each addition. Stir in the vanilla and salt, and then the flour.

4. Spread the dough into the prepared dish. Bake for 30 to 35 minutes, or until no depression remains when lightly touched in the center. Cool in the dish on a wire rack. When almost cool but still slightly warm, cut into 1×2-inch bars (4 across, 8 down). Roll the bars in powdered sugar to coat, knocking off any excess. Lay on waxed paper to cool completely.

❊ Chocolate Chip Brownies ❊

Some of the chocolate in this recipe is melted into the batter, the rest stirred in with the walnuts. The brownies are wonderful.

YIELD: 24 BROWNIES, EACH A 2-INCH SQUARE

½ cup (1 stick) unsalted butter
1½ cups granulated sugar
¼ cup milk
2 tablespoons vegetable oil
2 cups (12 ounces) semisweet chocolate morsels
1 tablespoon vanilla extract
4 large eggs
1½ cups all-purpose flour
½ teaspoon salt
½ teaspoon baking soda
1 cup chopped walnuts

1. Preheat the oven to 350°F. Grease a 12×9×2-inch baking dish.

2. In a large saucepan, bring the butter, sugar, milk, and oil to a boil. Remove from the heat. Add 1 cup of the chocolate morsels and stir until melted. Stir in the vanilla. Add the eggs, one at a time, beating well after each addition. Stir together the flour, salt, and baking soda; stir into the batter. Stir in the walnuts and the remaining 1 cup chocolate morsels.

3. Spread the batter evenly in the prepared baking dish. Bake for 28 to 30 minutes, or until the brownies are set around the edges and little or no depression remains when lightly touched in the center. Cool in the dish on a wire rack. When cool, cut into squares (4 across, 6 down).

❦ Peanut Butter Brownies ❦

The term *brownie* has come to mean any square bar cookie with the rich texture commonly associated with a chocolate brownie. These delectably fit that description.

YIELD: 24 BROWNIES, EACH A 2-INCH SQUARE

½ cup (1 stick) unsalted butter, softened
1 cup granulated sugar
1 cup firmly packed light brown sugar
1 cup creamy-style peanut butter
½ teaspoon salt
1 teaspoon vanilla extract
3 large eggs
1 cup all-purpose flour
1 cup (6 ounces) semisweet chocolate morsels

1. Preheat the oven to 350°F. Grease a 12×9×2-inch glass baking dish.

2. Beat together the butter and the granulated sugar until soft and creamy. Blend in the brown sugar, and then the peanut butter. Add the salt, vanilla, and eggs and beat until light and fluffy. Blend in the flour.

3. Spread the batter evenly in the prepared pan. Bake for 30 to 35 minutes, or until golden brown on top.

4. Remove from the oven and immediately sprinkle the chocolate morsels over the top of the brownies. Give them time to melt, and then spread evenly with a spatula. Cool in the pan on a wire rack. When cool, cut into 2-inch squares (4 across, 6 down).

❀ Frosted Peanut Butter Bars ❀

The combination of peanut butter and chocolate is seductive in these tender little cookie bars.

YIELD: 40 BARS, EACH 1½×2½ INCHES

½ cup (1 stick) unsalted butter, softened
½ cup granulated sugar
½ cup firmly packed light brown sugar
1 cup creamy peanut butter
1 teaspoon vanilla extract
1 large egg
1½ cups all-purpose flour
¼ teaspoon salt
1 teaspoon baking powder
2 cups (12 ounces) semisweet chocolate morsels
¾ cup chopped dry-roasted peanuts

1. Preheat the oven to 375°F. Lightly grease a 15½×10½×1-inch jelly roll pan.

2. Beat together the butter and granulated sugar until smooth and creamy. Add the brown sugar and beat again. Stir in the peanut butter, and then the vanilla and the egg. Stir together the flour, salt, and baking powder; stir into the butter mixture.

3. Drop globs of dough onto the prepared pan and pat into an even layer. Bake for 16 to 18 minutes, or until lightly browned on top.

4. Remove from the oven and immediately sprinkle the chocolate morsels over the top. Return to the oven and bake for 1 minute to soften the chocolate. Spread the chocolate with a small spatula. Sprinkle the peanuts over the chocolate and press in lightly. Cool in the pan, on a wire rack. When cool, cut into 1½×2½-inch bars (4 across, 10 down).

❀ Butterscotch Bars ❀

These are rich with butter, brown sugar, coconut, and bits of butterscotch. Mmmmm good.

YIELD: 70 SQUARES, EACH 1½ INCHES

1 cup (2 sticks) unsalted butter, softened
1½ cups firmly packed light brown sugar
2 large eggs
1 teaspoon vanilla extract
1¼ cups all-purpose flour
½ teaspoon salt
1 teaspoon baking soda
1 teaspoon ground cinnamon
2 cups quick or old-fashioned rolled oats (not instant)
1 cup sweetened flaked coconut
2 cups (12 ounces) butterscotch-flavored morsels

1. Preheat the oven to 375°F. Grease a 15½×10½×1-inch jelly roll pan.

2. Beat the butter until smooth and creamy. Add the brown sugar and beat again. Add the eggs, one at a time, beating well after each addition. Stir in the vanilla. Stir together the flour, salt, baking soda, and cinnamon; stir into the batter. Stir in the oats, coconut, and butterscotch morsels.

3. Spread the batter evenly in the prepared pan. Bake for 18 to 22 minutes, or until lightly browned on top. Cool in the pan on a wire rack. When cool, cut into squares (7 across, 10 down).

❊ Chocolate Chip Chocolate Squares ❊

This is an adaptation of the standard chocolate chip cookie recipe, baked into a bar and flavored with cocoa. They're very tasty.

YIELD: 48 SQUARES, EACH 1½ INCHES

½ cup (1 stick) unsalted butter, softened
¾ cup granulated sugar
1 large egg
½ teaspoon vanilla extract
1 cup all-purpose flour
2 tablespoons Dutch processed unsweetened cocoa powder
½ teaspoon baking soda
½ teaspoon salt
1 cup (6 ounces) semisweet chocolate morsels
½ cup chopped walnuts

1. Preheat the oven to 375°F. Grease a 12×9×2-inch baking dish.

2. Beat together the butter and sugar until smooth. Add the egg and vanilla and beat again. Stir together the flour, cocoa, baking soda, and salt; stir into the batter. Stir in the chocolate morsels and walnuts.

3. Drop globs of the dough into the prepared baking dish and spread evenly with a spatula or your fingertips. Bake for 13 to 15 minutes, or until set on the outside edges. Cool in the pan on a wire rack. When almost cool, cut into 1½-inch squares (6 across, 8 down).

❧ Hello Dollies ❧

Most layered cookies that are topped with a drizzle of sweetened condensed milk are simply too rich. These, on the other hand, although rich, invite you to come back for seconds.

YIELD: 54 BARS, EACH 1×2 INCHES

½ cup (1 stick) unsalted butter
1⅓ cups vanilla wafer crumbs
1 cup (6 ounces) semisweet chocolate morsels
1 cup sweetened flaked coconut
1 cup chopped pecans
1 can (14 ounces) sweetened condensed milk

1. Preheat the oven to 325°F. Place the butter in a 12×9×2-inch baking dish and place in the oven to melt while the oven is preheating.

2. As soon as the butter is melted, remove from the oven. Stir in the wafer crumbs with a fork. Spread the mixture evenly over the bottom of the pan and press gently into place with the back of the fork. Evenly sprinkle the chocolate morsels over the crust; add the coconut in a layer, and then the pecans. Drizzle the milk over all.

3. Bake for 25 to 30 minutes, or until browned around the edges. Cool in the dish on a wire rack. Wait for at least 2 hours before cutting into 1×2-inch bars (9 across, 6 down).

❧ Candy Bar Cookies ❧

These are rich and chewy with the flavor of a candy bar.

YIELD: 32 BARS, EACH 1½×2 INCHES

½ cup (1 stick) unsalted butter, softened
½ cup granulated sugar
½ cup firmly packed light brown sugar
1 teaspoon vanilla extract
1 large egg
1½ cups all-purpose flour
¼ teaspoon salt
½ teaspoon baking soda
1 package (6 ounces) almond brickle chips
1 cup (6 ounces) semisweet chocolate morsels

1. Preheat the oven to 375°F. Grease a 12×9×2-inch glass baking dish.

2. Beat the butter until smooth and creamy. Add both sugars and beat again. Add the vanilla and egg and beat again. Stir together the flour, salt, and baking soda; stir into the dough. Stir in the almond brickle chips.

3. Spread the dough evenly in the dish. Bake for about 20 minutes, or until golden brown on top. Sprinkle the chocolate morsels over the top and return to the oven for 1 minute. Spread the chocolate evenly over the top of the bars. When almost cool, cut into 1½×2-inch bars (4 across, 8 down).

❊ Apricot Squares ❊

I wanted to make an apricot filling for a bar cookie that started with dried apricots. But after repeated unsuccessful attempts to buy the apricots, I decided to try ready-made apricot preserves. I found that the preserves, freshened with a touch of fresh lemon juice, make an excellent filling.

YIELD: 48 SQUARES, EACH 1½ INCHES

1½ cups all-purpose flour
1½ cups quick or old-fashioned rolled oats (not instant)
1 cup firmly packed light brown sugar
¼ teaspoon salt
1 teaspoon baking powder
¾ cup (1½ sticks) unsalted butter, cut into 1-inch chunks
1½ cups apricot preserves or jam
1 teaspoon fresh lemon juice

1. Preheat the oven to 375°F. Use an ungreased 12×9×2-inch glass baking dish.

2. In a food processor, combine the flour, oats, brown sugar, salt, and baking powder and process just until mixed. Add the butter and process until coarse crumbs form. (Alternatively: Stir the dry ingredients together in a bowl. Cut in the butter with a pastry blender until coarse crumbs form.)

3. Press two-thirds of the crumb mixture over the bottom of the baking dish. Stir together the preserves and lemon juice. Spread the mixture over the

crust. Sprinkle the remaining crumbs over the top, and press in gently to make a smooth surface.

4. Bake for 30 to 35 minutes, or until browned on top. Cool in the pan on a wire rack. When cool, cut into 1½-inch squares (6 across, 8 down).

❀ Luscious Little Lemon Bars ❀

Here's a little yin/yang in a cookie: the chewiness and sweetness of the coconut against the creaminess and tang of the lemon filling. We love 'em.

YIELD: 16 SQUARES, EACH 2 INCHES

1 cup all-purpose flour
¼ cup powdered sugar
½ cup (1 stick) unsalted butter

FILLING:
2 large eggs
1 cup granulated sugar
grated zest of 1 lemon
¼ cup fresh lemon juice
½ teaspoon baking powder
2 tablespoons all-purpose flour
½ cup sweetened flaked coconut

1. Preheat the oven to 350°F.

2. In a food processor, combine the flour, powdered sugar, and butter and process to fine crumbs. (Alternatively: Stir the flour and powdered sugar together. Cut in the butter to make fine crumbs.) Pat the crumbs into an 8×8×2-inch glass baking dish. Bake the crust for 20 minutes.

3. To prepare the filling: Toward the end of the baking time for the crust, beat the eggs until smooth and lemon-colored. Beat in the sugar; stir in the lemon zest and lemon juice. Blend in the baking powder and flour. Stir in the coconut.

4. Pour the filling over the baked crust. Return to the oven and bake for 20 to 25 minutes, or until lightly browned on top. Cool in the baking dish on a wire rack. When cool, cut into 2-inch squares (4 across, 4 down). Refrigerate to store.

❀ Rosy Rhubarb Squares ❀

These were a surprise success. The recipe is based loosely on one for rhubarb cream pie. I like them even better than the pie.

YIELD: 16 SQUARES, EACH 2 INCHES

1¼ cups all-purpose flour
⅓ cup powdered sugar
½ cup (1 stick) unsalted butter, cut into 6 pieces

FILLING:
2 large eggs
1 cup granulated sugar
2 tablespoons all-purpose flour
¼ teaspoon baking powder
⅛ teaspoon salt
⅛ teaspoon ground nutmeg
2 cups diced rhubarb

1. Preheat the oven to 350°F.

2. In a food processor, combine the flour, powdered sugar, and butter and process to fine crumbs. (Alternatively: Stir the flour and powdered sugar together. Cut in the butter to make fine crumbs.) Reserve ½ cup of the crumbs for the topping. Press the remainder evenly in an 8×8×2-inch glass baking dish. Bake the crust for 12 minutes. Remove from the oven.

3. To prepare the filling: Beat the eggs with the granulated sugar until thick and smooth. Sprinkle on the flour, baking powder, salt, and nutmeg and stir to blend. Stir in the rhubarb.

4. Spoon the filling evenly over the partially baked crust. Sprinkle the reserved crumbs over the top. Bake for 35 to 40 minutes, or until browned on top. Cool in the pan on a wire rack. When cool, cut into 2-inch squares (4 down, 4 across). Refrigerate any leftovers.

❧ Cheesecake Squares ❧

When you want just a bite of cheesecake, these little squares hit the spot.
YIELD: 16 SQUARES, EACH 2 INCHES

1 cup all-purpose flour
2 tablespoons granulated sugar
2 tablespoons firmly packed light brown sugar
6 tablespoons (¾ stick) unsalted butter, softened
½ cup finely chopped walnuts

FILLING:
1 large package (8 ounces) plus 1 small package (3 ounces) cream cheese, softened
¼ cup plus 2 tablespoons granulated sugar
2 large eggs
1 tablespoon fresh lemon juice
1 teaspoon vanilla extract
1 teaspoon cornstarch
pinch of salt
½ cup sour cream.

1. Preheat the oven to 350°F.

2. In a food processor, combine the flour, both sugars, and the butter and process to fine crumbs. Add the walnuts and pulse to chop and mix. (Alternatively: Stir together the flour and both sugars. Cut in the butter to make fine

crumbs. Stir in the walnuts.) Reserve 1 cup of the crumbs for topping. Press the remaining crumbs evenly into an 8×8×2-inch glass baking dish. Bake the crust for 12 to 15 minutes, or until lightly browned. Remove from the oven.

3. To prepare the filling: In a food processor, process all of the cream cheese with the granulated sugar. Add the eggs and process until blended. Add the lemon juice, vanilla, cornstarch, and salt and process until smooth. Add the sour cream and pulse to mix. (Alternatively: With spoon or mixer, beat the ingredients together in the order given.)

4. Spread the filling over the baked crust. Sprinkle with the reserved crumbs. Bake for 35 to 40 minutes, or until the filling is set. Cool in the pan on a wire rack. Cover and chill for several hours or overnight. Cut into 2-inch squares (4 across, 4 down). Refrigerate to store.

❀ Praline Bars ❀

We had quite a discussion about whether to call these Brown Sugar Bars, Caramel Bars, or Praline Bars. The brown sugar gives the bars a caramel flavor, but it's the icing that will remind you of New Orleans and creamy pralines.

YIELD: 80 BARS, EACH 1×2 INCHES

2¼ cups all-purpose flour
1½ cups firmly packed light brown sugar
1 teaspoon salt
1 tablespoon baking powder
1 cup milk
½ cup (1 stick) unsalted butter
2 large eggs
1 teaspoon vanilla extract

ICING:
3 cups powdered sugar
1 cup finely chopped pecans
¾ cup firmly packed light brown sugar
6 tablespoons (¾ stick) unsalted butter
⅓ cup milk
pinch of salt

1. Preheat the oven to 400°F. Grease a 15½×10½×1-inch jelly roll pan.

2. In a large bowl, mix together the flour, brown sugar, salt, and baking powder. In a heavy saucepan, heat the milk and butter together until the milk is hot and the butter melts. Pour the milk/butter mixture over the dry ingredients and stir to mix. Add the eggs, one at a time, beating well after each addition. Stir in the vanilla.

3. Spread the batter in the prepared pan and bake for 20 minutes. Take from the oven and place on a wire rack. Immediately spread with the hot icing.

3. To prepare the icing: In a large bowl, mix the powdered sugar with the pecans. In a heavy saucepan, combine the brown sugar, butter, milk, and salt over medium-high heat. Cook until the butter melts and the milk bubbles. (Try to time this so that the milk mixture is ready to stir into the powdered sugar mixture as soon as the bars come out of the oven.) Stir the milk mixture into the powdered sugar mixture until well combined. Pour the icing over the hot bars, spreading evenly. When the bars are cool, cut into 1×2-inch bars (10 across, 8 down).

❄ Gingerbread Bars ❄

The gingerbread-spicy aroma that comes from the oven while these bars are baking is heavenly. The lemony icing is the perfect complement—they remind me of the hot gingerbread with lemon sauce I ate as a child. Be sure to measure the lemon juice for the icing accurately. Less than 4½ tablespoons will not produce a thin enough icing to soak slightly into the gingerbread, adding to its flavor; more than that will cause the icing to slide right off the top and overflow the pan.

YIELD: 60 BARS, EACH 1½×1¾ INCHES

3 cups all-purpose flour
1 cup granulated sugar
½ teaspoon salt
1 teaspoon baking soda
2 teaspoons ground ginger
1 teaspoon ground cinnamon
1 cup molasses
1 cup water
1 cup (2 sticks) unsalted butter
2 large eggs

ICING:
1 box (1 pound) powdered sugar
½ cup (1 stick) unsalted butter
4½ tablespoons fresh lemon juice

1. Preheat the oven to 400°F. Grease a 15½×10½×1-inch jelly roll pan.

2. In a large bowl, stir together the flour, sugar, salt, baking soda, ginger, and cinnamon. In a heavy saucepan, heat the molasses, water, and butter until the butter melts and the liquids are hot. Pour the butter mixture over the flour mixture and beat until fairly smooth; a few small lumps are okay. Add the eggs, one at a time, beating well after each addition.

3. Spread the batter in the prepared pan, taking care to fill the corners. Bake for 20 minutes. Remove the pan from the oven and place on a wire rack. Spread with the icing while still hot.

4. To prepare the icing: Place the powdered sugar in a large bowl. Heat the butter and lemon juice in a heavy saucepan until the butter melts and the lemon juice is hot. (Try to time this so that the butter mixture is ready to add to the sugar at about the time that the gingerbread bars come out of the oven.) Pour the butter mixture into the powdered sugar and beat until smooth. Pour the icing over the hot bars, spreading evenly. When cool, cut into 1½×1¾-inch bars (6 across, 10 down).

❧ Molasses Bars ❧

These are cake-like with the old-fashioned flavor of molasses. They're easy to make and provide a nice change from the usual fare.

YIELD: 32 BARS, EACH 1×2 INCHES

6 tablespoons (¾ stick) unsalted butter, softened
½ cup molasses
1 large egg
1 teaspoon vanilla extract
⅛ teaspoon salt
⅛ teaspoon baking soda
1 tablespoon hot water
1 cup all-purpose flour
sifted powdered sugar, for coating the bars

1. Preheat the oven to 375°F. Grease an 8×8×2-inch glass baking dish.

2. Beat the butter until smooth and creamy. Add the molasses and beat again. Add the egg, vanilla, and salt and beat again. Stir together the baking soda and hot water; stir into the batter. Stir in the flour.

3. Spread the batter evenly in the prepared baking dish. Bake for about 18 minutes, or until the bars just begin to pull away from the sides of the dish. Cool in the pan on a wire rack. While still slightly warm, cut into 1×2-inch bars (4 across, 8 down). Roll the bars in sifted powdered sugar to coat, knocking off any excess. Place on racks to cool completely.

❄ Southern Pecan Bars ❄

Easier to make than pecan pie, these chewy bars are a delight. I use a hint of rum for flavor. You can substitute 1½ teaspoons vanilla extract for the rum, if you prefer.

YIELD: 32 BARS, EACH 1½×2 INCHES

2 cups all-purpose flour
½ cup powdered sugar
1 cup (2 sticks) unsalted butter, softened

FILLING:
3 large eggs
1 cup granulated sugar
1 cup dark corn syrup
1 tablespoon dark rum
1 tablespoon all-purpose flour
2 tablespoons unsalted butter, melted
1½ cups chopped pecans

1. Preheat the oven to 350°F.

2. In a food processor, combine the flour, powdered sugar, and butter and process to fine crumbs. (Alternatively: In a medium bowl, stir together the flour and powdered sugar. Cut in the butter to make fine crumbs.) Firmly and

evenly press the dough into a 12×9×2-inch glass baking dish. Bake the crust for 15 minutes.

3. Meanwhile, prepare the filling: Beat the eggs with the granulated sugar. Add all of the remaining ingredients and mix well. Spread the filling evenly over the partially baked crust. Return to the oven and bake for 25 to 30 minutes, or until lightly browned on top. Cool in the pan on a wire rack. While still slightly warm, cut into 1½×2-inch bars (4 across, 8 down). Refrigerate to store.

❋ Sweet Dreams ❋

Ultra-rich Dream Bars have always been popular, but they are a bit too rich for my taste. I've reduced the sugar and butter content in my old recipe and renamed them Sweet Dreams.

YIELD: 24 BARS, EACH 1¼×2 INCHES

1 cup all-purpose flour
¼ cup firmly packed light brown sugar
4 tablespoons (½ stick) unsalted butter

FILLING:
2 large eggs
¾ cup firmly packed light brown sugar
1 teaspoon vanilla extract
½ teaspoon baking powder
1 tablespoon all-purpose flour
¼ teaspoon salt
1½ cups sweetened flaked coconut
½ cup chopped walnuts

FROSTING:
1 cup powdered sugar
1 tablespoon unsalted butter, softened
2 tablespoons fresh orange juice

1. Preheat the oven to 350°F.

2. In a food processor, combine the flour, ¼ cup brown sugar, and butter and process to fine crumbs. (Alternatively: Stir together the flour and brown sugar. Cut in the butter to make fine crumbs.) Press into an 8×8×2-inch glass baking dish. Bake the crust for 20 minutes.

3. Meanwhile, prepare the filling: In a mixing bowl, beat the eggs until smooth and lemon-colored. Beat in the ¾ cup brown sugar. Blend in the vanilla, baking powder, flour, and salt. Stir in the coconut and walnuts. Pour the filling over the partially baked crust. Return to the oven and bake for 25 to 30 minutes longer, or until browned on top. Cool in the pan on a wire rack while you prepare the frosting.

4. To prepare the frosting: In a small bowl, blend the powdered sugar with the softened butter. Stir in the orange juice to make a pourable frosting. Drizzle the frosting evenly over the bars while they are still warm. When cool, cut into 1¼×2-inch bars (4 across, 6 down).

❊ SHAPED COOKIES ❊

There's a little "mud-pie" artist in us all. Exercise your talents with some tasty cookie doughs.

❋ Old-Fashioned Vanilla Sugar Cookies ❋

Sugar cookies can be made in various ways—dropped from a spoon (see Soft Sugar Cookies, page 25), flattened with a sugar-coated glass, or rolled out and cut with cookie cutters. Here, they are molded into little sugar-coated balls and flattened with a fork.

YIELD: 4 DOZEN 2½-INCH COOKIES

2 cups all-purpose flour
1 cup plus 3 tablespoons granulated sugar
½ teaspoon salt
½ teaspoon baking powder
½ teaspoon baking soda
⅛ teaspoon ground nutmeg
½ cup (1 stick) unsalted butter
1 large egg
2 tablespoons heavy (whipping) cream
¾ teaspoon vanilla extract

1. Stir together the flour, 1 cup of the sugar, the salt, baking powder, baking soda, and nutmeg. Cut in the butter to make fine crumbs.

2. In a small measuring cup, beat the egg with the cream and vanilla until smooth. Make a well in the dry ingredients and pour in the egg mixture. Work in the flour mixture with a wooden spoon, using your hands at the last, if necessary.

3. Gather the dough into a ball, wrap tightly in plastic wrap, and refrigerate for about 20 minutes, or until firm enough to shape. Meanwhile, preheat the oven to 350°F. Use ungreased baking sheets.

4. Place the remaining 3 tablespoons sugar in a small bowl. Roll the dough into 1-inch balls. Roll in the sugar to coat. Place the balls on the baking sheets, leaving 2 inches between the balls. Dip a fork in flour, shake off any excess, and flatten the balls of dough with the tines. Repeat, dipping the fork in flour as needed to prevent sticking. Bake for 9 to 11 minutes, or until golden on top. Transfer to wire racks to cool.

❧ Another Sugar Cookie ❧

The recipe for these was sent to me by my cousin Bernice, who got it from her friend Irene—you know how it goes. I have made several changes, for which, I trust, I am forgiven. Half a recipe can be made quite easily, but I don't advise it. They are so good and go so fast, you'll run out much too soon if you don't make the full amount.

YIELD: 6 DOZEN 2½-INCH COOKIES

1 cup (2 sticks) unsalted butter, softened
1 cup solid vegetable shortening
about 1½ cups granulated sugar
1 cup powdered sugar
2 teaspoons vanilla extract
2 large eggs
4 cups all-purpose flour
¼ teaspoon salt
1 teaspoon baking soda
1 teaspoon cream of tartar

1. Preheat the oven to 350°F. Lightly grease 2 baking sheets, or use non-stick pans.

2. Beat the butter and shortening together until smooth and creamy. Beat in 1 cup of the granulated sugar until smooth and creamy. Add the powdered sugar and beat again. Add the vanilla and beat well. Add the eggs, one at a

time, beating well after each addition. Stir together the flour, salt, baking soda, and cream of tartar; add to the batter in 4 parts, mixing well after each addition.

3. Place ⅓ to ½ cup of granulated sugar in a shallow plate. Dip out a hunk of dough with a teaspoon and gently roll into a ball with the palms of your hands. The ball should measure between 1¼ and 1½ inches in diameter. The dough will be soft. Roll it gently to keep it from compacting. (If the dough is too soft to handle, cover and chill for about half an hour and try again.) Roll each ball in the granulated sugar and place on a baking sheet, leaving 3 inches between the balls. Repeat until 12 balls are made. Press the balls gently with a fork that has been dipped in sugar. Bake in the preheated oven for 13 to 15 minutes, or until lightly browned on top. Transfer to wire racks to cool.

❧ Yankee Doodles ❧

These remind me of snickerdoodles without the cinnamon. I like them better.

YIELD: 5 DOZEN 2¼-INCH COOKIES

1 cup (2 sticks) unsalted butter, softened
1¼ cups granulated sugar
1 large egg
½ teaspoon vanilla extract
2¼ cups all-purpose flour
½ teaspoon salt
2 teaspoons baking soda
1 teaspoon cream of tartar

1. Beat the butter with 1 cup of the sugar until smooth and creamy. Add the egg and vanilla and beat again. Stir together the flour, salt, baking soda, and cream of tartar; stir into the batter. Cover the bowl of dough with plastic and refrigerate until firm enough to shape, about 30 minutes.

2. Meanwhile, preheat the oven to 350°F. Use ungreased baking sheets.

3. Place the remaining ¼ cup sugar in a small bowl. Roll the dough into 1-inch balls. Roll in sugar to coat. Place on the baking sheet, allowing 3 inches between the balls. Bake in the preheated oven for 10 to 12 minutes, or until golden on top. Transfer to wire racks to cool.

❋ Best Little Butter Cookies ❋

A good butter cookie should be very tender and not overly sweet. These fill the bill perfectly. I like to use them as my "plain" cookie in a gift box of assorted kinds.

YIELD: 4 DOZEN 1½-INCH COOKIES

1 cup (2 sticks) unsalted butter, softened
1 cup sifted powdered sugar (be sure to sift before measuring)
1½ teaspoons vanilla extract
½ teaspoon almond extract
2 cups all-purpose flour
¼ teaspoon baking powder
¼ teaspoon salt

1. Preheat the oven to 350°F. Use ungreased baking sheets.

2. In a mixing bowl, beat the butter with the sifted powdered sugar until smooth and creamy. Blend in both extracts. Stir together the flour, baking powder, and salt; blend into the creamed mixture in 3 parts.

3. Roll spoonfuls of the dough into 1-inch balls. Place the balls on the baking sheets, leaving 3 inches between the balls. (If the dough is too soft to handle, cover with plastic wrap, and refrigerate for 15 to 20 minutes to firm.) Flatten the cookies gently in a crisscross pattern, using a fork dipped in flour. Dip

the fork before each pressing, knocking off any excess flour before use. Bake for
10 to 12 minutes, or until the cookies are very lightly browned on top. Cool on
wire racks.

❈ Jelly Dots ❈

These jelly-filled cookies will melt in your mouth.

YIELD: 5 DOZEN 1½-INCH COOKIES

1 cup (2 sticks) unsalted butter, softened
½ cup plus about 3 tablespoons granulated sugar
2 large egg yolks
1 teaspoon vanilla extract
¼ teaspoon salt
2½ cups all-purpose flour
about ⅓ cup currant or crabapple jelly, for filling the cookies

1. Beat the butter until smooth and creamy. Add ½ cup of the sugar and beat again. Stir in the egg yolks, and then the vanilla and salt. Stir in the flour. Cover and chill the dough for 30 to 60 minutes, or until firm enough to handle.

2. Preheat the oven to 375°F. Use ungreased baking sheets.

3. Place about 3 tablespoons of granulated sugar in a small bowl. Pinch off hunks of the dough and roll into 1-inch balls. Roll the balls in sugar to coat. Place on the baking sheets, leaving 2 inches between the balls. Using your forefinger or the handle of a wooden spoon dipped in sugar, make deep indentations in each ball.

4. Bake for 9 to 11 minutes, or until the bottoms of the cookies are lightly browned and the tops are firm; the tops will remain pale in color. Transfer to wire racks to cool. Fill each indentation with about ¼ teaspoon of the jelly.

❀ Chocolate-Raspberry Thumbprints ❀

Don't you love the flavor combination of chocolate and raspberries? It's perfect in these fudgy thumbprint cookies.

YIELD: 4 DOZEN 1½-INCH COOKIES

½ cup (1 stick) unsalted butter
2 squares (1 ounce each) unsweetened chocolate
½ cup granulated sugar
½ cup firmly packed light brown sugar
½ teaspoon vanilla extract
1 large egg
2 cups all-purpose flour
½ teaspoon baking powder
¼ teaspoon salt
about 1 tablespoon powdered sugar
about ¼ cup raspberry jam

1. In a glass bowl, microwave the butter with the chocolate on high power for 1 to 1½ minutes. Stir to finish melting the chocolate. (Alternatively: Melt the chocolate with the butter in a heavy saucepan over low heat, stirring constantly. Transfer to a bowl.) Add both sugars and beat until blended. Stir in the vanilla and egg. Stir together the flour, baking powder, and salt; blend into the chocolate mixture. Cover the bowl and chill the dough until firm, about 2 hours.

2. Preheat the oven to 350°F. Use ungreased baking sheets.

3. Working with about one-fourth of the dough at a time, knead the dough until pliable. Shape into 1⅛-inch balls and place on the baking sheets, leaving 2 inches between the balls. With your thumb or forefinger, make a deep indentation in the top of each ball.

4. Bake for 6 to 8 minutes, or until little or no depression remains when lightly touched; they should not brown. Transfer to wire racks until almost cool.

5. When almost cool, dust lightly with the powdered sugar (a sieve works best). Fill each indentation with about ¼ teaspoon of the raspberry jam.

❄ Best-Ever Meltaways ❄

These are the epitome of the melt-in-your-mouth cookie. The little bit of cornstarch used makes them extra-tender, and a touch of almond extract rounds out
the flavor.

YIELD: 4 DOZEN 1½-INCH COOKIES

1 cup (2 sticks) unsalted butter, softened
½ cup powdered sugar
1 teaspoon vanilla extract
¼ teaspoon almond extract
¼ teaspoon salt
2 cups all-purpose flour
2 tablespoons cornstarch
½ cup sifted powdered sugar, for coating the cookies

1. Beat the butter with the unsifted powdered sugar until smooth and
creamy. Add both extracts and the salt and beat again. Stir together the flour and
cornstarch; stir into the dough. Cover the bowl with plastic and chill for 1 hour,
or until firm enough to shape.

2. Preheat the oven to 325°F. Use ungreased baking sheets.

3. Pinch off hunks of the dough and roll into 1-inch balls. Place on the
baking sheets, leaving 2 inches between the balls. Bake for 15 to 18 minutes, or
until set; the cookies will not color. Let cool on the pans until cool enough to

handle. Roll the cookies in sifted powdered sugar to coat. Lay on waxed paper to cool. Roll again in sifted powdered sugar when cool.

Chocolate Meltaways

Follow the recipe for Best-Ever Meltaways. Substitute ¼ cup Dutch-processed unsweetened cocoa powder for ¼ cup of the flour in the recipe.

❀ Jam-Filled Cookie Tarts ❀

Cookie tarts were one of my mother's specialties. Whenever she came to visit, she made her tarts and tea sandwiches, and we invited friends for coffee. These are a snap to make. Simply press the dough into the pan and fill with ready-made jam. Be sure not to underbake them, however, or you'll never get them out of the pan in one piece.

YIELD: 16 COOKIE TARTS

½ cup (1 stick) unsalted butter, softened
⅓ cup granulated sugar
1 large egg yolk
⅛ teaspoon salt
¼ teaspoon vanilla extract
¼ teaspoon lemon extract
1 cup plus 2 tablespoons all-purpose flour
about ½ cup apricot jam

1. Preheat the oven to 350°F. Lightly grease 16 miniature muffin cups (1 inch deep, 1½ inches across) even if you're using nonstick pans.

2. In a mixing bowl, beat together the butter and sugar until smooth and creamy. Beat in the egg yolk, and then the salt and both extracts. Stir in the flour.

3. Divide the dough into 4 equal parts, and then divide each of those parts into 4 equal parts. Drop each part into a muffin cup, and press to line the muffin cup with the dough. The pastry should be ¼ inch thick. (At first it may

look like you have too much dough, but it compresses as you shape it.) Drop about ½ tablespoon of the jam into each dough-lined cup.

4. Bake for 20 to 25 minutes, or until the top edges of the crust are well browned. Let the pans sit on a wire rack for about 1½ minutes. Then, with the aid of a small fork, carefully lift out the tarts and let cool completely on a wire rack.

❀ Biscotti ❀

Biscotti are Italian cookies that are baked twice—first as a loaf, and then again, when sliced. They have a crisp texture and a pleasant sweetness that invites after-dinner munching.

YIELD: 32 BISCOTTI

1 cup slivered almonds
3 large eggs
1 teaspoon vanilla extract
1 cup granulated sugar
¼ cup (½ stick) unsalted butter, melted and cooled
2½ cups all-purpose flour
¼ teaspoon salt
1 teaspoon baking soda

1. Toast the almonds in a dry skillet over medium heat, stirring often, until golden. Watch carefully, lest they burn. Set aside to cool.

2. Preheat the oven to 325°F. Lightly grease 1 baking sheet, or use a nonstick pan.

3. Beat the eggs with the vanilla until smooth. Add the sugar and beat until thick. Stir in the melted butter. Stir together the flour, salt, and baking soda; stir into the batter. Stir in the toasted almonds.

4. Turn out the dough onto a lightly floured surface and toss until no longer sticky. Knead lightly once or twice and divide the dough in half. Shape each half into a rectangle about 2 inches wide and 12 to 13 inches long. Place them side by side on the same baking sheet, leaving 2 inches between the loaves.

5. Bake for 35 to 40 minutes, or until lightly browned. Transfer to a wire rack and let cool for 10 minutes. Reduce the oven temperature to 275°F.

6. Cut the loaves diagonally into ¾-inch slices. Arrange the slices flat on 2 ungreased baking sheets. Bake one sheetful at a time for 10 minutes. Turn the biscotti over and bake for 10 minutes on the second side. Transfer to wire racks to cool.

❧ Crunchy Peanut Butter Cookies ❧

We prefer these peanut butter cookies when they're made with creamy peanut butter and just a touch of honey. I add chopped nuts for the crunch. Why not use chunky peanut butter instead, you say? Because the cookies aren't as good.

YIELD: 5 DOZEN 2-INCH COOKIES

½ cup (1 stick) unsalted butter, softened
1 cup granulated sugar
1 cup creamy peanut butter
1 large egg
½ teaspoon vanilla extract
1 tablespoon honey
1½ cups all-purpose flour
½ teaspoon salt
½ teaspoon baking soda
½ teaspoon baking powder
1 cup finely chopped dry-roasted peanuts

1. Preheat the oven to 375°F. Use ungreased baking sheets.

2. Beat the butter and sugar together until smooth and creamy. Beat in the peanut butter, and then the egg, vanilla, and honey. Stir together the flour, salt, baking soda, baking powder, and nuts; stir into the dough.

3. Roll the dough into 1¼-inch balls and place on ungreased baking sheets, leaving 2 inches between the balls. Flatten the balls with a fork dipped in sugar. Bake for 8 to 10 minutes, or until lightly browned on top. Let the cookies cool on the pan for 1 minute. Transfer to wire racks to cool completely.

❈ Crisscross Peanut Butter Cookies ❈

These peanut butter cookies will literally melt in your mouth.

YIELD: 3 DOZEN 2½-INCH COOKIES

½ cup solid vegetable shortening
½ cup granulated sugar
½ cup firmly packed light brown sugar
1 cup creamy peanut butter
1 large egg
1½ teaspoons vanilla extract
1 tablespoon milk
1½ cups all-purpose flour
½ teaspoon salt
½ teaspoon baking powder
½ teaspoon baking soda

1. Preheat the oven to 375°F. Use 2 ungreased baking sheets.

2. Beat the shortening with both sugars until creamy. Beat in the peanut butter, and then the egg, vanilla, and milk. Stir together the flour, salt, baking powder, and baking soda; stir into the dough.

3. Roll the dough into 1¼-inch balls and place on the baking sheets, leaving 2 inches between the balls. Flatten each ball crisscross fashion with a fork dipped in flour. Bake for 10 to 12 minutes, or until very lightly browned on top. Let the cookies cool on the pan for 1 minute. Transfer to wire racks to cool completely.

❊ Peanut Butter Kisses ❊

I know of no one who can resist these delectable cookies. The combination of peanut butter and sweet chocolate is hard to beat.

YIELD: 5 DOZEN 2-INCH COOKIES

½ cup (1 stick) unsalted butter
½ cup firmly packed light brown sugar
about ¾ cup granulated sugar
½ cup creamy peanut butter
1 teaspoon vanilla extract
1 large egg
1⅓ cups plus 1 tablespoon all-purpose flour
¼ teaspoon salt
½ teaspoon baking powder
½ teaspoon baking soda
60 milk chocolate kisses, unwrapped

1. Preheat the oven to 350°F. Use 2 ungreased baking sheets.

2. Beat the butter with the brown sugar and ½ cup of the granulated sugar until smooth and creamy. Beat in the peanut butter, and then the vanilla and egg. Stir together the flour, salt, baking powder, and baking soda; stir into the dough.

3. Place about ¼ cup of granulated sugar in a small bowl. Shape the dough into 1-inch balls. Roll in the granulated sugar to coat, and place on the baking sheets, leaving 2 inches between the balls.

4. Bake for 10 to 12 minutes, or until golden. Remove from the oven and immediately press a milk chocolate kiss into the top of each hot cookie. Transfer to wire racks to cool.

❀ Sugar 'n' Spice Cookies ❀

These crisp sugar cookies have a gentle spiciness that will invite you to take "just one more."

YIELD: 3½ DOZEN 2½-INCH COOKIES

½ cup solid vegetable shortening
½ cup granulated sugar
½ cup firmly packed light brown sugar
1 large egg
1½ teaspoons vanilla extract
1½ cups all-purpose flour
¼ teaspoon salt
½ teaspoon baking soda
½ teaspoon ground cinnamon
½ teaspoon ground allspice
¼ teaspoon ground ginger
¼ teaspoon ground nutmeg

1. Beat the shortening and both sugars together until smooth and creamy. Beat in the egg and vanilla. Stir together the flour, salt, baking soda, cinnamon, allspice, ginger, and nutmeg; stir into the dough.

2. Gather the dough into a ball, cover with plastic wrap, and chill until firm enough to shape, about 30 minutes.

3. Meanwhile, preheat the oven to 375°F. Lightly grease 2 baking sheets, or use nonstick pans.

4. Scoop out the dough with a spoon and shape into 1-inch balls. Place them on the baking sheets, leaving 2 inches between the balls. Dip a flat-bottomed glass in sugar, and use it to flatten the balls until ¼ inch thick.

5. Bake for 7 to 9 minutes, or until the edges are golden brown. Transfer to wire racks to cool.

❀ Ginger Gems ❀

These are similar to gingersnaps, but not as highly flavored. I believe I like them better.

YIELD: 5 DOZEN 2-INCH COOKIES

¾ cup vegetable shortening
½ cup firmly packed light brown sugar
¾ cup granulated sugar
¼ cup molasses
1 large egg
2 cups all-purpose flour
¼ teaspoon salt
2 teaspoons baking soda
1 teaspoon ground ginger
1 teaspoon ground cinnamon

1. Preheat the oven to 350°F. Use ungreased baking sheets.

2. Beat the shortening with the brown sugar and ½ cup of the granulated sugar until well blended. Add the molasses and beat again. Stir in the egg. Stir together the flour, salt, baking soda, ginger, and cinnamon; stir into the dough.

3. Place ¼ cup of granulated sugar in a small bowl. Roll the dough into 1-inch balls. Roll the balls in the sugar to coat. Place on the baking sheets, leaving 2 inches between the balls.

4. Bake for 10 to 12 minutes, or until hardly any depression remains when the cookies are lightly touched in the center. Transfer to wire racks to cool.

❁ Brown Sugar Shortbread ❁

Serve these with homemade ice cream for a special dessert.

YIELD: 16 WEDGES

½ cup (1 stick) unsalted butter, softened
¼ cup firmly packed light brown sugar
⅛ teaspoon salt
¼ teaspoon vanilla extract
1 ¼ cups all-purpose flour

1. Preheat the oven to 325°F. Use an ungreased baking sheet.

2. Beat the butter with the brown sugar until well blended. Add the salt and vanilla and beat again. Stir in the flour.

3. Gather the dough into a ball and slice the ball in half. Place the halves, cut-sides down, on either end of the baking sheet. Press out each portion into a 4½-inch circle. Using the edge of a dull knife, score each circle into 8 equal wedges. Using the tines of a fork, pierce the dough along the score lines, making sure the fork goes through to the baking sheet. Gently press a decorative edge around the circumference of each circle with the tips of the tines held flat. Press gently so as not to make the edge thinner than the rest of the dough.

4. Bake for 25 minutes, or until the shortbread is pale ivory in color and the edges are lightly browned. Cool slightly on the pan. As soon as the shortbread is cool enough to handle, cut or break apart along the score lines. Cool the individual wedges on wire racks.

❊ REFRIGERATOR COOKIES ❊

Having a roll of ready to slice and bake cookie dough in the refrigerator is almost as important as having money in the bank. It certainly makes an impression on my grandchildren.

❀ Vanilla Refrigerator Cookies ❀

I shape most of my refrigerator cookies as is described here—in a rectangular log rather than a round one. They are easier to shape and can be stacked easily in the refrigerator. For baking, I cut them ³⁄₁₆ inch thick, halfway between ⅛ and ¼ inch. The smaller cut is not quite thick enough to keep them from burning; the larger cut makes a cookie that's not as crisp as I like.

YIELD: 4 DOZEN 2½-INCH COOKIES

½ cup (1 stick) unsalted butter, softened
1 cup granulated sugar
1 large egg
1½ teaspoons vanilla extract
1¼ cups all-purpose flour
¼ teaspoon salt
1½ teaspoons baking powder

1. Beat the butter until smooth and creamy. Add the sugar and beat again. Add the egg and vanilla and beat again. Stir together the flour, salt, and baking powder; stir into the dough. Cover the bowl of dough and chill until firm enough to shape, 30 to 60 minutes.

2. Divide the dough in half. Shape each half into a rectangular log, 1½ inches on a side and 4½ inches long. Wrap each log in waxed paper and refrigerate until firm, at least 4 hours, or for as long as 3 days.

3. When ready to bake, preheat the oven to 400°F. Use ungreased baking sheets.

4. Cut the logs into 3/16-inch slices. Place the slices 1 inch apart on the baking sheets. Bake for 6 to 8 minutes, or until lightly browned. Transfer to wire racks to cool.

Walnut Refrigerator Cookies

Follow the recipe for Vanilla Refrigerator Cookies. Add ½ cup chopped walnuts to the dough before the first chilling. Proceed as before.

❧ Butterscotch Refrigerator Cookies ❧

Here's a basic cookie with a rich, brown sugar flavor.

YIELD: 4 DOZEN 2½-INCH COOKIES

½ cup (1 stick) unsalted butter, softened
1 cup firmly packed light brown sugar
1 large egg yolk
½ teaspoon vanilla extract
¼ teaspoon salt
½ teaspoon baking soda
2 tablespoons hot water
1¾ cups all-purpose flour

1. Beat the butter until soft and creamy. Add the brown sugar and beat again. Add the egg yolk, vanilla, and salt and beat again. Stir together the baking soda and hot water; stir into the dough. Stir in the flour. Cover the bowl of dough with plastic and chill until firm enough to shape, 30 to 60 minutes.

2. Divide the dough in half. Shape each half into a rectangular log, 1½ inches on a side and 4½ inches long. Wrap each log in waxed paper and refrigerate until firm, at least 4 hours, or for as long as 3 days.

3. When ready to bake, preheat the oven to 400°F. Use ungreased baking sheets.

4. Cut the logs into ³⁄₁₆-inch slices. Place the slices 1 inch apart on the baking sheets. Bake for 6 to 8 minutes, or until lightly browned. Transfer to wire racks to cool.

Butter-Pecan Cookies

Follow the recipe for Butterscotch Refrigerator cookies. Add ½ cup chopped pecans to the dough before the first chilling. Proceed as before.

❀ Chocolate Chippers ❀

Keep these handy so you can pop them in the oven right before supper. Serve them warm, with vanilla ice cream, for dessert.

<small>YIELD: 3 DOZEN 2½-INCH COOKIES</small>

½ cup (1 stick) unsalted butter, softened
1 cup granulated sugar
1 large egg
1 teaspoon vanilla extract
1½ tablespoons milk
1½ cups all-purpose flour
¼ cup Dutch-processed unsweetened cocoa powder
½ teaspoon salt
1½ teaspoons baking powder
1 cup (6 ounces) semisweet chocolate morsels
½ cup chopped walnuts

1. Beat the butter until smooth and creamy. Add the sugar and beat again. Beat in the egg. Stir in the vanilla and milk. Stir together the flour, cocoa, salt, and baking powder; stir into the dough. Stir in the chocolate morsels and walnuts. Cover the bowl of dough with plastic and chill until firm enough to shape, 30 to 60 minutes.

2. Divide the dough in half. Shape each half into a rectangular log, 2 inches on a side and 4½ inches long. Wrap each in waxed paper and refrigerate until firm, at least 8 hours, or for as long as 3 days.

3. When ready to bake, preheat oven to 375°F. Use ungreased baking sheets.

4. Cut the logs into ¼-inch slices. Place the slices on the baking sheets, leaving 1½ inches between the slices. Bake for 8 to 10 minutes, or until only a little depression remains when the cookies are lightly touched in the center. Transfer to wire racks to cool.

❀ Granny's Icebox Cookies ❀

Every grandmother should have a batch of these in her refrigerator or freezer.
Each roll bakes into 2 dozen fresh, hot cookies.

YIELD: 8 DOZEN 2¼-INCH COOKIES

½ cup (1 stick) unsalted butter, softened
½ cup solid vegetable shortening
1 cup granulated sugar
1 cup firmly packed light brown sugar
2 large eggs
1 teaspoon vanilla extract
3¼ cups all-purpose flour
½ teaspoon salt
1 teaspoon baking soda
1 teaspoon cream of tartar

1. Beat the butter and shortening together until smooth and creamy.
Beat in the granulated sugar, and then the brown sugar. Add the eggs, one at a
time, beating well after each addition. Blend in the vanilla. Stir together the flour,
salt, baking soda, and cream of tartar; stir into the dough.

2. Divide the dough into 4 equal parts. Roll each part into a 1½×6-inch
round log. (If the dough is too soft to roll, cover and chill for 30 to 60 minutes
and try again.) Wrap each log in waxed paper or plastic wrap and refrigerate until
firm, at least 8 hours, or for as long as 3 days.

3. When ready to bake, preheat the oven to 350°F. Lightly grease 2 baking sheets, or use nonstick pans.

4. Cut the logs into ¼-inch slices and place on the baking sheets, leaving 2 inches between the slices. Bake for 9 to 11 minutes, or until lightly browned. Transfer to wire racks to cool.

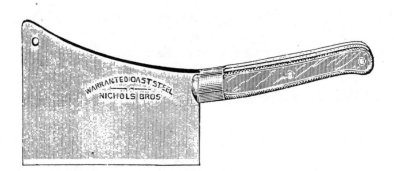

❄ Peanut Butter Slices ❄

These are tender, melt-in-your-mouth cookies with a peanut butter flavor that's hard to beat.

YIELD: 4 DOZEN 2×2½-INCH COOKIES

½ cup (1 stick) unsalted butter, softened
½ cup granulated sugar
½ cup firmly packed light brown sugar
¾ cup creamy peanut butter
1 large egg
1 teaspoon vanilla extract
1½ cups all-purpose flour
½ teaspoon salt
½ teaspoon baking powder
½ teaspoon baking soda

1. Beat the butter until smooth and creamy. Add both sugars and beat again. Stir in the peanut butter. Add the egg and vanilla and beat again. Stir together the flour, salt, baking powder, and baking soda; stir into the dough. Cover the bowl of dough with plastic and chill until firm enough to shape, 30 to 60 minutes.

2. Divide the dough in half. Shape each half into a rectangular log, 1½ inches high and 2 inches wide. Wrap each log in waxed paper and refrigerate until firm, at least 4 hours, or for as long as 3 days.

3. When ready to bake, preheat the oven to 375°F. Use ungreased baking sheets.

4. Cut the logs into ¼-inch slices. Place the slices on the baking sheets, leaving 1½ inches between the slices. Bake for 8 to 10 minutes, or until lightly browned on top. Transfer to wire racks to cool.

Crunchy Peanut Butter Slices

Follow the recipe for Peanut Butter Slices. Add ¾ cup chopped dry-roasted peanuts to the dough before the first chilling. Proceed as before.

❀ Oatmeal Refrigerator Cookies ❀

These have the nutty flavor of oatmeal in a chewy little cookie.

YIELD: 3 DOZEN 2½-INCH COOKIES

½ cup (1 stick) unsalted butter, softened
½ cup granulated sugar
½ cup firmly packed light brown sugar
1 large egg
¼ teaspoon vanilla extract
¼ teaspoon almond extract
1 cup all-purpose flour
½ teaspoon salt
½ teaspoon baking soda
1½ cups old-fashioned or quick-cooking rolled oats (not instant)

1. Beat the butter until smooth and creamy. Add both sugars and beat again. Add the egg and both extracts and beat again. Stir together the flour, salt, baking soda, and oats; stir into the dough. Cover the bowl of dough and chill until firm enough to shape, 30 to 60 minutes.

2. Divide the dough in half. Shape each half into a rectangular log, 1½ inches on a side and 4½ inches long. Wrap each log in waxed paper. Refrigerate until firm, at least 4 hours, or for as long as 3 days.

3. When ready to bake, preheat the oven to 375°F. Use ungreased baking sheets.

4. Cut the logs into ¼-inch slices. Place the slices 1 inch apart on the baking sheets. Bake for 7 to 9 minutes, or until lightly browned. Let sit on the baking sheets for about 10 seconds, and then transfer to wire racks to cool.

❀ Coconut Crisps ❀

These are tender-crisp and filled with sweet coconut.

YIELD: 4 DOZEN 2½-INCH COOKIES

½ cup (1 stick) unsalted butter, softened
½ cup granulated sugar
½ cup firmly packed light brown sugar
1 large egg
1 teaspoon vanilla extract
1½ cups all-purpose flour
¼ cup cornstarch
¼ teaspoon salt
1½ teaspoons baking powder
1⅓ cups sweetened flaked coconut

1. Beat the butter until soft and creamy. Add both sugars and beat again. Add the egg and vanilla and beat again. Stir together the flour, cornstarch, salt, and baking powder; stir into the dough. Stir in the coconut. Cover the bowl of dough with plastic and chill until firm enough to shape, 30 to 60 minutes.

2. Divide the dough in half. Shape each half into a rectangular log, 1½ inches on a side and 4½ inches long. Wrap each log in waxed paper. Refrigerate until firm, at least 4 hours, or for as long as 3 days.

3. When ready to bake, preheat the oven to 375°F. Use ungreased baking sheets.

4. Cut the logs into ³⁄₁₆-inch slices. Place the slices 1 inch apart on the baking sheets. Bake for 8 to 10 minutes, or until lightly browned. Transfer to wire racks to cool.

❀ Toffee Swirls ❀

Of all the toffee cookies I make, these are the most popular. They have a rich butter and brown sugar base with a filling of semisweet chocolate. The same dough can be used to make Toffee Bars. Simply spread the dough in a greased 15½×10½×1-inch jelly roll pan and bake at 350°F for 15 to 20 minutes, or until lightly browned; sprinkle with the chocolate, and spread when melted.

YIELD: 5 DOZEN 2×2½-INCH COOKIES

1 cup (2 sticks) unsalted butter, softened
1 cup firmly packed light brown sugar
1 large egg yolk
1 teaspoon vanilla extract
⅛ teaspoon salt
2 cups all-purpose flour
1 cup (6 ounces) semisweet chocolate morsels

1. Beat the butter until smooth and creamy. Add the brown sugar and beat again. Add the egg yolk, vanilla, and salt and beat again. Stir in the flour. Cover the bowl of dough with plastic and chill until firm, about 1 hour.

2. Place the chocolate morsels in a glass measuring cup and microwave on high for 1 to 1½ minutes. (Alternatively: Melt in a double boiler over hot water.)

3. On a lightly floured surface, roll out the dough to a 12×15-inch rectangle. Trim any uneven edges. Spread the melted chocolate over the dough,

stopping ¼ inch from the edges. Allow the cold dough to firm up the chocolate. Starting with a 15-inch side, roll up the dough to form a log. Cut the log in half across the middle. Wrap each log in waxed paper. Refrigerate until firm, at least 4 hours, or for as long as 3 days.

4. When ready to bake, preheat the oven to 350°F. Use ungreased baking sheets.

5. Cut the logs into ¼-inch slices. Place the slices on the baking sheets, leaving 2 inches between the slices. Bake for 10 to 12 minutes, or until lightly browned on top. Let rest for about 1 minute before transferring to wire racks to cool.

❧ Brown Sugar Gingerbread Rounds ❧

These have the richness of butter and brown sugar with just enough molasses and
ginger to echo old-fashioned gingerbread cookies. The same dough can be used
to make Gingerbread Boys and Girls: Simply cover the dough and chill for 2
hours. On a lightly floured surface, roll out ¼ inch thick; cut with boy- and
girl-shaped cutters, and bake at 350°F for 10 to 15 minutes.

YIELD: 2½ DOZEN 2¾-INCH COOKIES

½ cup (1 stick) unsalted butter, softened
¾ cup firmly packed light brown sugar
¼ cup molasses
1 large egg
2 cups all-purpose flour
¼ teaspoon salt
½ teaspoon baking powder
½ teaspoon baking soda
1 teaspoon ground ginger
1 teaspoon ground cinnamon

1. Beat the butter until smooth and creamy. Add the brown sugar and
beat again. Add the molasses and egg and beat again. Stir together the flour, salt,
baking powder, baking soda, ginger, and cinnamon; stir into the dough. Cover
the bowl of dough with plastic and chill until firm enough to shape, 30 to 60
minutes.

2. Divide the dough in half. Roll each half into a 2-inch round log. Wrap in waxed paper. Chill until firm, at least 4 hours, or for as long as 3 days.

3. When ready to bake, preheat the oven to 350°F. Use lightly greased or nonstick baking sheets.

4. Cut the logs into ¼-inch slices. Place the slices on the baking sheets, leaving 1 inch between the slices. Bake for 10 to 12 minutes, or until only a little depression remains when the cookies are lightly touched in the center. Transfer to wire racks to cool.

❊ CUTOUT COOKIES ❊

Collect a variety of cutters and have fun rolling and cutting out dough for fanciful cookies. It's a wonderful way to make cookies with a child. Each of these recipes lists a preferred size and baking time. If your cookies are larger or smaller than mine, you will have to adjust the baking time (longer for larger cookies, shorter for smaller ones). For best results, stay close to the original.

❀ Sugar Babies ❀

These sugar-coated sugar cookies are crisp and delicious.

YIELD: 7 DOZEN 1¾-INCH COOKIES

6 tablespoons (¾ stick) unsalted butter
¼ cup plus 2 tablespoons vegetable shortening
1¼ cups granulated sugar
2 large eggs
1 teaspoon vanilla extract
2½ cups all-purpose flour
1 teaspoon salt
1 teaspoon baking powder

1. Beat the butter and shortening together until smooth and creamy. Add 1 cup of the sugar and beat again. Add the eggs, one at a time, beating well after each addition. Stir in the vanilla. Stir together the flour, salt, and baking powder; stir into the dough. Cover and chill for 1 hour to firm.

2. Read about Rolling Out Cookie Dough, page 16. Preheat the oven to 375°F. Use ungreased baking sheets.

3. Place the remaining ¼ cup sugar in a small bowl. Working with half of the dough at a time and on a lightly floured surface, roll out the dough ³⁄₁₆ inch thick. Cut with a 1¾-inch cookie cutter. Place the cookies in the sugar, turning

them once to coat both sides. Place on the baking sheets, leaving 1 inch between the cookies. Bake for 8 to 10 minutes, or until the edges are browned. Transfer to wire racks to cool.

❀ Lemon Sugar Cookies ❀

These are very simple—and very good. The thin coating of lemon-flavored glaze is divine. Lay back in the hammock and enjoy one with a glass of iced tea.

YIELD: ABOUT 2 DOZEN 3¼-INCH COOKIES

zest of ½ lemon
1 cup granulated sugar
½ cup (1 stick) unsalted butter, softened
1 large egg
2 tablespoons fresh lemon juice
2 cups all-purpose flour
½ teaspoon baking soda
⅛ teaspoon salt

GLAZE:
1 cup powdered sugar
1 tablespoon unsalted butter, softened
1 to 2 tablespoons fresh lemon juice

1. Remove the zest of ½ lemon with a swivel peeler or lemon zester. In a food processor, combine the zest with the granulated sugar and process until finely shredded. In a bowl, beat the lemon sugar with the butter until blended. (Alternatively: Grate the zest of ½ lemon with a fine grater. Add to the butter with the sugar.) Blend in the egg, and then the lemon juice. Stir together the

flour, baking soda, and salt; stir into the butter mixture. Cover and chill until the dough is firm, about 1 hour.

2. Read about Rolling Out Cookie Dough, page 16. Preheat the oven to 350°F. Use ungreased baking sheets.

3. Working with half of the dough at a time and on a lightly floured surface, roll out the dough ¾₆ inch thick. Cut with a 3-inch round cookie cutter and place on the baking sheets, leaving 1 inch between the cutouts. Bake for 10 to 12 minutes, or until very little depression remains when the cookies are gently touched in the center. Transfer to wire racks to cool to room temperature.

4. To prepare the glaze: Mix the powdered sugar, butter, and 1 tablespoon of the lemon juice. Add enough additional lemon juice to make the mixture spreadable with a pastry brush. Coat the tops of the cooled cookies with the glaze.

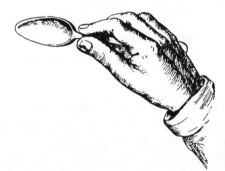

❋ Brown Sugar Cutouts ❋

These are slightly chewy cookies with a brown sugar taste that whispers of molasses.

YIELD: 2½ DOZEN 3-INCH COOKIES

½ cup (1 stick) unsalted butter, softened
1½ cups firmly packed light brown sugar
1 teaspoon vanilla extract
2 large eggs
2½ cups all-purpose flour
¼ teaspoon salt
½ teaspoon baking powder
¼ teaspoon baking soda

1. Beat the butter until smooth and creamy. Add the brown sugar and beat again. Add the vanilla and eggs and beat again. Stir together the flour, salt, baking powder, and baking soda; stir into the dough. Cover and chill the dough until firm, about 2 hours.

2. Read about Rolling Out Cookie Dough, page 16. Preheat the oven to 350°F. Lightly grease 2 baking sheets, or use nonstick pans.

3. Working with half of the dough at a time and on a lightly floured surface, roll out the dough ¼ inch thick. Cut with a 2½-inch cookie cutter and place on the baking sheets, leaving 1½ inches between the cookies. Bake for 10 to 12 minutes, or until browned on the edges. Transfer to wire racks to cool.

❋ Molasses Sugar Cookies ❋

These are lightly flavored with molasses and spice. They are particularly good with a glass of cold milk.

YIELD: 2 DOZEN 3-INCH COOKIES

½ cup (1 stick) unsalted butter, softened
¾ cup plus 2 tablespoons granulated sugar
¼ cup molasses
1 large egg
2 cups all-purpose flour
½ teaspoon salt
1 teaspoon baking soda
1 teaspoon ground cinnamon
1 teaspoon ground ginger

1. Beat the butter until soft and creamy. Add ¾ cup of the sugar and beat again. Add the molasses and egg and beat again. Stir together the flour, salt, baking soda, cinnamon, and ginger; stir into the dough. Cover and chill until firm, about 1 hour.

2. Read about Rolling Out Cookie Dough, page 16. Preheat the oven to 375°F. Use ungreased baking sheets.

3. Working with half of the dough at a time and on a lightly floured surface, roll out the dough ¼ inch thick. Cut out with a 2½-inch cookie cut-

ter and place on the baking sheets, leaving 1½ inches between the cookies. Sprinkle the tops of the cookies with some of the remaining 2 tablespoons sugar. Bake for 8 to 10 minutes, or until browned on the edges. Transfer to wire racks to cool.

❧ Powdered Sugar Cookies ❧

The powdered sugar gives these a tender-crisp, almost melt-in-your-mouth qual-
ity. If you've taken up tea, you'll want to serve these with your next pot.

YIELD: 6½ DOZEN 2-INCH COOKIES

1 cup (2 sticks) unsalted butter, softened
1½ cups powdered sugar, plus additional for sifting over the cookies
1 large egg
1 teaspoon vanilla extract
2½ cups all-purpose flour
¼ teaspoon salt
1 teaspoon baking soda
1 teaspoon cream of tartar

1. Beat the butter until smooth and creamy. Add 1½ cups of the powdered sugar and beat again. Add the egg and vanilla and beat again. Stir together
the flour, salt, baking soda, and cream of tartar; stir into the dough. Cover and
chill until firm, about 2 hours.

2. Read about Rolling Out Cookie Dough, page 16. Preheat the oven to
375°F. Use ungreased baking sheets.

3. Working with one-third of the dough at a time and a lightly floured
surface, roll out the dough ³⁄₁₆ inch thick. Cut with a 1¾-inch cookie cutter and

place on the baking sheets, leaving 1 inch between the cookies. Stir the additional powdered sugar through a fine-mesh sieve over the tops of the cookies, coating them lightly but evenly. Bake for 7 to 8 minutes, or until browned on the edges. Transfer to wire racks to cool.

❧ Sour Cream Sugar Cookies ❧

These have just enough sour cream in the dough to add a flavorful tang. They're a definite must for your sugar-cookie repertoire.

YIELD: 2 DOZEN 3¼-INCH COOKIES

½ cup (1 stick) unsalted butter, softened
1 cup granulated sugar, plus additional for sprinkling on top
1 large egg
1½ teaspoons vanilla extract
¼ cup sour cream
2¼ cups all-purpose flour
¼ teaspoon salt
¼ teaspoon baking soda
1 teaspoon baking powder

1. Beat the butter until smooth and creamy. Add 1 cup of the sugar and beat again. Add the egg and vanilla and beat again. Stir in the sour cream. Stir together the flour, salt, baking soda, and baking powder; stir into the dough. Cover and chill until firm, about 1 hour.

2. Read about Rolling Out Cookie Dough, page 16. Preheat the oven to 350°F. Lightly grease 2 baking sheets, or use nonstick pans.

3. Working with half of the dough at a time, roll out the dough ³⁄₁₆ inch thick. Cut with a 3-inch cookie cutter and place the cookies on the baking sheets,

leaving 1 ½ inches between them. Sprinkle the cookies lightly but evenly with additional sugar. Bake for 8 to 10 minutes, or until browned on the edges. Transfer to wire racks to cool.

❀ Peanut Butter Sugar Cookies ❀

These have the texture of a sugar cookie and the flavor of a peanut butter cookie, with a sprinkling of sugar to top it all off.

YIELD: 2½ DOZEN 3-INCH COOKIES

½ cup (1 stick) unsalted butter, softened
½ cup creamy peanut butter
½ cup firmly packed light brown sugar
½ cup granulated sugar, plus additional for sprinkling on top
1 large egg
1 teaspoon vanilla extract
1¾ cups all-purpose flour
½ teaspoon salt
½ teaspoon baking powder
½ teaspoon baking soda

1. Beat the butter and peanut butter together until smooth and creamy. Add the brown sugar and ½ cup of the granulated sugar and beat again. Add the egg and vanilla and beat again. Stir together the flour, salt, baking powder, and baking soda; stir into the dough. Cover and chill until firm, about 1 hour.

2. Read about Rolling Out Cookie Dough, page 16. Preheat the oven to 350°F. Use ungreased baking sheets.

3. Working with half of the dough at a time, roll out the dough ³⁄₁₆ inch thick. Cut with a 2½-inch cookie cutter and place on the baking sheets, leaving 1½ inches between the cookies. Sprinkle the cookies lightly with the additional sugar. Bake for 10 to 12 minutes, or until browned on the edges. Transfer to wire racks to cool.

❧ Christmas Cookies ❧

These are lightly flavored with rum, making them a special Christmas treat. They can be cut out with Christmas cookie cutters, such as trees and angels, if you wish. Adjust the baking time to allow for any difference in the size of the cookies.

YIELD: 2½ DOZEN 3¼-INCH COOKIES

½ cup (1 stick) unsalted butter, softened
1 cup granulated sugar, plus additional for sprinkling
1 large egg
1 tablespoon vanilla extract
1 tablespoon dark rum
1 tablespoon milk
2 cups all-purpose flour
¼ teaspoon salt
1 teaspoon baking powder

1. Beat the butter until soft and creamy. Add 1 cup of the sugar and beat again. Add the egg and beat again. Stir in the vanilla, rum, and milk. Stir together the flour, salt, and baking powder; stir into the dough. Cover and chill until firm, about 1 hour.

2. Read about Rolling Out Cookie Dough, page 16. Preheat the oven to 375°F. Use ungreased baking sheets.

3. Working with one-third of the dough at a time and on a lightly floured surface, roll out the dough to ⅛ inch thick. Cut with a 3-inch cookie

cutter and place on the baking sheets, leaving 1½ inches between them. Sprinkle a light, even coating of the additional sugar on the tops of the cookies. Bake for 6 to 8 minutes, or until browned on the edges. Transfer to wire racks to cool.

❦ Sweet Cinnamon Crisps ❦

These tender little cookies are flavored inside and out with sweet cinnamon sugar. They are absolutely addictive.

YIELD: 7 DOZEN 2-INCH COOKIES

1½ cups granulated sugar
1 tablespoon ground cinnamon
1 cup (2 sticks) unsalted butter, softened
2 large eggs, 1 of them separated
1 teaspoon vanilla extract
2½ cups all-purpose flour
1 teaspoon baking powder
½ teaspoon salt
1 teaspoon cool water

1. In a large bowl, stir together the sugar and cinnamon. Reserve ¼ cup of the cinnamon-sugar mixture for topping the cookies. Add the butter to the bowl and beat with the cinnamon-sugar until well blended. Add the whole egg and the egg yolk and mix well. Add the vanilla and blend well. Stir together the flour, baking powder, and salt; stir into the dough. Cover and chill the dough until firm enough to roll out, 20 to 30 minutes.

2. Read about Rolling Out Cookie Dough, page 16. Preheat the oven to 400°F. Use ungreased baking sheets.

3. Working with one-third of the dough at a time, roll out slightly less than ¼ inch thick. Cut with a 1¾-inch round cookie cutter and place on the baking sheets, leaving 2 inches between the cutouts.

4. Mix the egg white with the cool water. Brush the top of each cookie with the egg wash, and sprinkle with a little less than ⅛ teaspoon of the reserved cinnamon-sugar. Bake for 7 to 9 minutes, or until browned on the edges. Transfer to wire racks to cool.

❆ Little Butter Crisps ❆

It's hard to stop eating these once you start. I especially like them with chocolate ice cream.

YIELD: 5 DOZEN 1¾-INCH COOKIES

½ cup (1 stick) unsalted butter, softened
¾ cup granulated sugar
1 large egg
1 teaspoon vanilla extract
1 teaspoon milk
1½ cups all-purpose flour
¼ teaspoon salt
¼ teaspoon baking powder

1. Beat the butter and sugar together until well blended. Beat in the egg, and then the vanilla, and then the milk. Stir together the flour, salt, and baking powder; stir into the dough. Cover with plastic wrap and chill until firm, about 1 hour.

2. Read about Rolling Out Cookie Dough, page 16. Preheat the oven to 375°F. Use ungreased baking sheets.

3. Working with one-third of the dough at a time and on a lightly floured surface, roll out the dough ⅛ inch thick. Cut with a 1¾-inch round

cookie cutter and place on the baking sheets, leaving 1 inch between the cutouts. Bake for 5 to 7 minutes, or until the edges are lightly browned. Transfer to wire racks to cool.

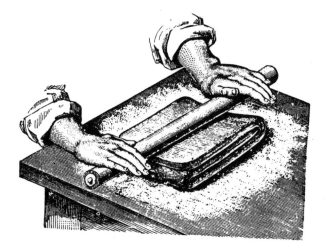

❈ Cream Cheese Crisps ❈

The secret to making these cookies lies in rolling out the dough as thin as cardboard. That's what makes them crisp.

YIELD: 5 DOZEN 2½-INCH COOKIES

½ cup (1 stick) unsalted butter, softened
1 small package (3 ounces) cream cheese, softened
1 cup granulated sugar
1 large egg
1 teaspoon vanilla extract
1 tablespoon milk
2 cups all-purpose flour
¼ teaspoon salt
¼ teaspoon baking soda
¼ teaspoon baking powder

1. Beat together the butter and cream cheese until soft and creamy. Add the sugar and beat again. Add the egg and vanilla and beat again. Stir in the milk. Stir together the flour, salt, baking soda, and baking powder; stir into the dough. Cover and chill until firm, about 2 hours.

2. Read about Rolling Out Cookie Dough, page 16. Preheat the oven to 375°F. Use ungreased baking sheets.

3. Working with one-fourth of the dough at a time and on a lightly floured surface, roll out the dough slightly less than ⅛ inch thick. Cut with a 2½-inch cookie cutter and place on the baking sheets, leaving 1 inch between the cookies. Bake for 8 to 10 minutes, or until lightly browned on top. Transfer to wire racks to cool.

❋ Cornmeal Cookies ❋

If you like cornmeal in your bread and crackers, you'll love these cookies. They are crunchy-crisp and rich with butter, sugar, and cornmeal goodness.

YIELD: 2½ DOZEN 3½-INCH COOKIES

1 cup (2 sticks) unsalted butter, softened
1 cup granulated sugar
1 teaspoon vanilla extract
1 large egg
1½ cups all-purpose flour
1 cup yellow cornmeal
¼ teaspoon salt
1 teaspoon baking powder

1. Beat the butter until soft and creamy. Add the sugar and beat again. Add the vanilla and egg and beat again. Stir together the flour, cornmeal, salt, and baking powder; stir into the dough. Cover and chill until firm enough to roll out, about 1 hour.

2. Read about Rolling Out Cookie Dough, page 16. Preheat the oven to 350°F. Use ungreased baking sheets.

3. Working with half of the dough at a time, roll out ³⁄₁₆ inch thick. Cut with a 3-inch cookie cutter and place on the baking sheets, leaving 1½ inches between the cookies. Bake for 11 to 13 minutes, or until golden brown. Transfer to wire racks to cool.

❀ Old-Fashioned Buttermilk Cookies ❀

These are like the ones your grandmother—no, your great-grandmother—used to bake for filling lunch boxes. They're not too sweet, with the evocative flavors of buttermilk and nutmeg combined.

YIELD: 9 DOZEN 2-INCH COOKIES

½ cup (1 stick) unsalted butter, softened
½ cup vegetable shortening
1½ cups granulated sugar
2 large eggs
2 teaspoons vanilla extract
4 cups all-purpose flour
½ teaspoon salt
1½ teaspoons baking soda
½ teaspoon ground nutmeg
½ cup buttermilk

1. Beat the butter and shortening until smooth and creamy. Add the sugar and beat again. Add the eggs and vanilla and beat again. Stir together the flour, salt, baking soda, and nutmeg. Add the dry ingredients to the dough alternately with the buttermilk (3 parts dry, 2 parts buttermilk), until well mixed. Cover the dough and chill until firm, about 2 hours.

2. Read about Rolling Out Cookie Dough, page 16. Preheat the oven to 350°F. Use ungreased baking sheets.

3. Working with one-fourth of the dough at a time, roll out ¼ inch thick. Cut with a 1¾-inch cookie cutter and place on the baking sheets, leaving 1 inch between the cookies. Bake for 10 to 12 minutes, or until lightly browned on top. Transfer to wire racks to cool.

❧ Mumsley's Animal Crackers ❧

I loved animal crackers when I was growing up. My mother would give me my own circus wagon boxful, and I could dole them out to myself as I pleased. I decided to make a homemade version, and I like them better than any from a box. They're perfect for when the grandchildren come to visit.

YIELD: 3 TO 6 DOZEN COOKIES, DEPENDING ON SIZE

½ cup solid vegetable shortening
½ cup granulated sugar
¼ cup firmly packed light brown sugar
1 teaspoon vanilla extract
2 large eggs
2½ cups all-purpose flour
2 teaspoons baking powder
1 teaspoon Dutch processed unsweetened cocoa powder
½ teaspoon salt

1. Beat together the shortening and both sugars until blended. Blend in the vanilla. Add the eggs, one at a time, blending well after each addition. Stir together the flour, baking powder, cocoa, and salt; stir into the dough. Gather the dough into a ball, wrap tightly with plastic wrap, and refrigerate until firm, 1 to 2 hours.

2. Read about Rolling Out Cookie Dough, page 16. Preheat the oven to 375°F. Use ungreased baking sheets.

3. Work with one-fourth of the dough at a time; keep the remaining dough covered and chilled. On a lightly floured surface, roll out the dough slightly less than ¼ inch thick. Cut with your choice of animal cookie cutters (circus animals, barnyard animals, or dinosaurs). Place on the baking sheets, leaving 2 inches between the cutouts. Bake for 8 to 12 minutes, depending on size, or until the edges are lightly browned. Transfer to wire racks to cool.

❊ INDEX ❊